A Free Church Perspective:

A Study in Ecclesiology

by
Stewart A. Newman

WITHDRAWN

STEVENS BOOK PRESS

Wake Forest, North Carolina

A FREE CHURCH PERSPECTIVE:
A Study in Ecclesiology

Copyright © 1986 by Stewart A. Newman
All rights reserved

ISBN 0-913029-12-2

Library of Congress Cataloging-in-Publication Data
Newman, Stewart A.
  A free church perspective.

  Bibliography: p.
  1. Church.   2. Free churches.   I. Title.
BV600.2.N494 1986   262'.4   86-6055
ISBN 0-913029-12-2 (pbk.)

STEVENS BOOK PRESS
P.O. Box 71
Wake Forest, NC 27587
Telephone 919-556-3830

Printed in the USA

Contents

To Sara and her Jewels:
Her Sons
Charles Virgil
S. Albert, Jr.
Harvey Knupp

Foreword

The title, A Free Church Perspective, has been chosen to reflect the open and often unpredictable spontaneity of those who observe ecclesiological polity under free church auspices. The author, during more than thirty-five years of classwork in the discipline, has endeavored to define the basic principle of free churchism and then explore the articulation of this principle in the associations and functions of the religion.

The topics of this study do not represent lectures on the subject. Classwork was never conducted on the basis of lectures. It consisted rather in discussions engaged in by teacher and students and this work represents the summary judgments arrived at during these discussions. The author brought to the classwork an inclusive range of bibliographical material the composite of which is reflected in these studies. Few of the background sources are indicated specifically but all are acknowledged to exist as the source springs of the author's judgments herein recorded.

The author brought to the study a background of having been reared within the polity of free churchism and has worked for fifty years in educational institutions under free church direction.

The manuscript has been read in its entirety by Dr. Lee Gallman, Dr. Carl Johnson and Cedric Hepler to whom indebtedness is acknowledged for many valuable suggestions during its development.

I

Introduction

This is an analysis and interpretation of what has come to be known as the free church movement, a tradition which arose in the wake of the Reformation, which has come more recently to have considerable influence in twentieth century Christian circles. The Anabaptists of the post-Reformation era are said to have been the source spring of free churchism. Contemporary groups whose origins are traceable directly to the Anabaptists are negligible in number but their ideas are identifiable in many quarters. Perhaps, among the major modern communions who have incorporated most extensively the free church perspective should be listed the Disciples of Christ, the Baptists and the Congregationalists.

It is fair to say that in the historical development of all contemporary communions each has become an admixture of churchly traditions. Even those groups which lie closest to the original free church outlook have long since adapted their manner of life to elements of traditional ecclesiology. There is considerable advantage, therefore, in addressing a study of this kind to an examination of the basic perspective of the free church movement rather than attempting to analyze the point of view of any particular contemporary church.

At the outset it is well to note that the use of the term, free church, is to be distinguished carefully from the more general use of the term with reference to groups which maintain their work apart from government support and direction. For example, in Great Britain, and in several countries on the Continent, where churches are "established," that is, are maintained as departments of government, the churches in these countries which are maintained apart from government connection are also called free churches.

The churches being studied here are, in the main, free in this sense also. They rarely occur under the auspices of government. There are a few exceptions. For example, due to circumstances peculiar to American Colonial life, the Congregationalists became the established church of Massachusetts, an arrangement which prevailed until 1834, years after the separation of church and state had been defined by the Constitution of the United States.

The churches of the post-Reformation tradition establish their work in the context of a different concept of freedom. They introduced what is sometimes called a "humanizing" factor in the equation. In a sense peculiar to themselves they involve the individual in the processes of religious life.

We are indebted to Franklin Littell for a detailed account of the beginnings of the movement. In his judgment the Anabaptists did not serve merely as an addendum to the Reformation. Instead, their emphasis was upon "a new concept of a community of disciples." (Franklin Hamlin Littell, *The Free Church*. Boston: Star King Press, 1957, p. 1) Although definitely sympathetic with the Reformers in their divergence from the medieval church, we shall observe that they intended to go considerably beyond Luther and Calvin in their application of the Protestant principle. The Anabaptists insisted on the freedom and responsibility of the individual as being central in all matters of faith, beginning with human participation in revelation and becoming articulate in the voluntary aspects of association in church membership.

It may be that these are not the best of times for the church, nor the faith itself. As a matter of fact, there is substance to the notion, expressed in some quarters, that the church itself is the chief hindrance to Christian faith in our time. This is the judgment of many who are sympathetically involved in the religion, as well as an impression entertained by a gainsaying world which continues to heap upon the church an impressive degree of indifference.

This is by no means a unanimous opinion, to be sure. Now, as in the past, a large company of the devout is gratified by the complexion of life which it finds in the churchly enterprise. Normally, persons of this persuasion are not given to critical attitudes. They are seldom drawn into a consideration of the church's prospect beyond the level of its relative prosperity. Understandably, these are annoyed by any question regarding the legitimacy of the churchly enterprises.

On the surface, to think of the church in any sense as being a hindrance to religion is to be judged as being negatively censorious. It is calculated, also, to enlist at once the sentiment of the anti-church community, those who for one reason or another oppose the values which are traditionally associated with religion.

When such a remark is heard frequently among conscientious churchmen, however, it warrants a more careful consideration. At least it deserves to be examined in the context of a professed regard for the wellbeing of the Judaeo-Christian faith, as paradoxical as these judgments appear to be.

From many quarters is heard the opinion that the current church is in crisis. In whatever specific terms that crisis is identified it is grave, witness the extent to which the religion engages in what it calls "renewal." The multiplicity of its efforts in that direction is tacit admission that much that the religion is, or is doing, is missing the mark. Even the casual observer perceives that its influence on the general cultural pattern is embarrassingly small. Its diminution began during the Renaissance in developments which deprived it of its central place in Western civilization, a predicament which, progressively, it has suffered since that time.

If for no other reason the twentieth century church would be wallowing in a veritable sea of crises because of the multiplicity of forms through which, in the modern era, it seeks to present its claims. The babel of voices with which it speaks creates a mass of confusion which, in turn, is reflected in the character of its existential entity as well as in a blurred vision of its mission.

The major communions have not been altogether insensitive to this state of affairs. This lack of togetherness has prompted innumerable attempts at reunification. During the first half of the twentieth century widespread movements in this direction were pursued but with limited success. As a matter of fact, the processes of the church's dismemberment have often more than kept pace with its concern for corporate solidarity so that the net losses have sometimes exceeded its gains.

The obstacles to reunion have been formidable. For example, each group came to the ecumenical discussions with deep loyalties to doctrinal commitments which, in many instances, were centuries old. These theological variations are often slight but they have served well to rationalize group independence. The minutiae of customs, also engrained by long usage, have proved to be very difficult to alter. Not the least obstacle to those seeking mergers has been the jealous regard for the institutional investments which each party has accumulated. By all accounts ecumenicity has suffered miserably at the hands of its friends as well as it detractors so that it has managed to achieve little apparent success. The Christian world is poised to enter the twenty-first century still largely characterized by its habitual confusion. Its image continues to be that of a miserably fragmented enterprise, with its strength as well as its sincerity severely compromised.

However, as discouraging as has been the schismatic condition of organized religion for several centuries past there are encouraging signs upon the horizon. For one thing, the various communions which, in most instances, from the time of their inception have been encapsulated in separate operations, by the exigencies of more recent circumstances are being forced into closer contact with each other.

Developments of this order are not difficult to explain. It is a phenomenon generally characteristic of our age. At no point in the past have individuals or societal structures been more generously exposed to each other than in this century. Demographic processes have created a heavy population density in most areas making it necessary for people to live much more closely together. It becomes increasingly difficult for anyone to arrange a life-style of isolation, to pursue a course of peculiar separateness.

In church circles this has created surprising degrees of inclusiveness, even in provinces which have heretofore been rigidly exclusive. For example, within the aura of Vatican II Augustin Cardinal Bea addressed himself, with apparent enthusiasm, to all other Christians as "our separated brethren." (Augustin Cardinal Bea, *Unity in Freedom*. New York: Harper and Row, 1964.)

It is evident that the farther into the complexities and interdependencies of the modern era the major Christian bodies go in pursuit of what they have taken to be their distinctive ways the more clearly they discern that those around them deserve a more constructive respect than they have been willing to bestow upon them. Besides, the more contacts are established the more largely all parties discover that much of what those around them believe and practice as churches is essentially the same as they in their separateness have been maintaining. These agreements are being discovered often enough to warrant the expectation that the sometimes hostile, always indifferent attitudes of the past will subside, that a more sympathetic rapport is a reasonable prospect.

While by the inexorable pressures of modernity segments of the Christian community are being compelled to acknowledge mutually respectable associations, by these same processes another strange consequence is becoming prominent. With increasing frequency free church ideas are beginning to emerge as a common denominator of the religious outlook. In the light of the groundswell of change which was created by the Renaissance this is not unexpected. In medievalism mankind had been bound by ancient fetters of authoritarianism. Whatever else Renaissance meant, it ushered in modernity and modernity meant for the individual a great deal of liberation. Man as a person was thrust into broader and more responsible dimensions of effort and achievement.

This change continues to seep into the inner precincts of religion. Even the most staid patterns of the faith are being reconstructed in its light. As we shall have occasion to observe in detail when we come to deal specifically with the alteration of patterns of authority, theologians are now beginning to overhaul the divine-human ratios of ultimacy. Human beings are now being recognized as qualified by nature to participate for themselves in matters of the eternal; being thus qualified they cannot escape the duty to enter creatively into choices which are determinitive of both conduct and destiny.

There is no thought here that these recent developments in the several churches have come about by the influence of the free church movement as such. For one thing, the movement began and has re-

mained relatively small within the total Christian
community. It has scarcely ever been large enough
nor has it been actively vocal enough to have been
that influential. One is inclined to think, instead, that
when the rise of the free churches is accounted for it
will become apparent that these same trends in the
larger body are to be explained in the same manner
as one accounts for the free churches, namely, by the
leavening action of the environing circumstance in
which both have occurred.

Normally, there are present in any cultural situation factors sufficient to determine largely the direction of people's thoughts and actions. By the acci-
dents of history these factors strike more directly at
some than at others, resulting in wide differences
in the time and place of their consequence. In this
instance it is evident that some small groups were
less restrained by their past and, therefore, were able
to react more quickly to the cultural climate than did
others. It would seem that these small sixteenth
century free churchmen managed, somehow, to in-
culcate into their perspective, more essentially than
the rest, the spirit which more recently has changed
all of Western civilization from medievalism into
modernity.

Perhaps due to an inherent individualism in the
character of the free church movement, churches of
this persuasion, with some notable exceptions, have
not been encouraging to ecumenical interests. As a
matter of fact, this feature of their general outlook
may have caused them to contribute more than their
proportionate share to the fragmentation of Christianity in recent decades. However, when there begins
to emerge definite signs of the free church spirit in

broad areas of the church, generally, these otherwise individualistic groups can scarcely fail to be impressed. The less mature will welcome the sign as an indication that the Christian world is making preparation "to join their church." To say the least, such signs warrant a serious re-examination of the roots of free churchism and its correlative symptoms in the broader precincts of church life. It may be that the free churches will be seen, not as indelibly impressed with certain creative aspects of the gospel, as to have been generated by the same atmosphere which more recently has come to prevail in the culture as a whole.

The background of the author chanced to be that of a communion whose roots are loosely related to the original free church movement. This orientation has been significant solely in encouraging him to be sympathetic with the issues of the Renaissance which have come to be identified as "modernity." Occupation with the modern mind has, in turn, encouraged an interest in developments which have been directly consequent to this modern mood. Insights gathered from this perspective have become the straight-edge against which contemporary religious movements are being assessed.

Indebtedness to many minds of many communions is acknowledged, especially the many who have been and are wrestling with the issues which have been thrust upon the Christian world by the circumstances of our time. We are especially indebted to the succeeding generations of students who participated in lively discussions of the perspective here being examined, who patiently permitted us to "try on them" the ideas herein discussed and who made

creative contribution to the development of the
point of view.

The analysis will entail a review of the historical
context out of which radical departures such as the
free church movement emerged. It will engage in a
detailed examination of the whole concept of authority which became the touchstone of their endeavor.
It will survey the implications of their basic concepts
for the ramifications of their religious thought and
activity. It will include topics such as the basis for
membership, their manner of organization, official
leadership, rituals and their corporate endeavor
called denominationalism.

II

The Cultural Context of Free Churchism

It is a truism of history that societal structures do not exist in a vacuum. Institutions exert a certain influence upon their surroundings and, in turn, are affected by their surroundings. Those who are familiar with the growth and development of the Christian movement understand the significance of this principle. The religion contributed immensely to Western culture, arising from obscurity within it and, in the course of a millennium, becoming the dominant institution of the society. Like a river it altered measurably the channel through which it flowed while at the same time it acquired increasingly the color of its banks.

It is on this account that the context within which free churches arose becomes significant. The groups occurred at a point in human affairs within a circumstance which also had been prepared by the exigencies of earlier developments. It would be difficult to think that churches like the free churches could have emerged under conditions other than those with which they were surrounded in the sixteenth century. Therefore, it is to a brief review of the development of these historical conditions that this study is now directed.

11

The church and its development are a prime example of the molding processes of culture. By the pressures of the environment in which it grew, in both doctrinal affirmation and in organizational function, the church was changed into a posture antithetical to that with which it began. That posture corresponded almost *in toto* with the culture in which it existed. From a simple, folk level of concern it became a complex, hierarchical system, called the medieval church.

The revolutionary changes which occurred in Europe in the fifteenth and sixteenth centuries altered the course of all aspects of life in the region. It is significant to this study, therefore, to examine the developments which produced medievalism, on the one hand, and the environmental changes which eventually transformed medievalism into modernity.

In another connection the author has traced in detail these developments. Here we are chiefly occupied with the principal characteristics of medievalism as they furnished the background of the Renaissance and the modernity which inspired such movements as the free churches. These churches can be said to have been true children of their times.

On the basis of this theory of cultural influence, if one takes into account "the way the world wags" at any given time he is able to explain in considerable degree the changes which have come to the religious institution. The changes which occurred in the church are a prime example of the operation of the principle. The church claims a divine source for the ideas and purposes it embraces but the manner of its life in the world is no exception to this rule of cultural influence. Its societal structure is largely determined by the cultural factors which weigh constantly upon it.

Of all the "wagging ways" of the ancient world two were conspicuous in their impact upon the Christian movement. For one thing, the atmosphere of the era was supercharged with authoritarianism. Autocracy was embodied in strong empires over the entire Mediterranean basin, empires which were constantly competing with each other for advantaged positions. The aggrandizement of wealth and power was the occupation of the few at the expense of the many. Christianity had its inception at a time when societal order was established almost universally on the basis of the disfranchisement and privation of the masses, an order which maintained itself by the habitual submissiveness of the populace. To that point it seems not to have occurred to many that there were conditions other than that of abject tyranny as the human prospect. For the majority all aspects of experience were determined by forces above and beyond the individual's understanding or control. It is noteworthy, in passing, that the early devotees of the religion were recruited mainly from among those who enjoyed little of the managerial dimensions of the culture.

These were the conditions under which from an early period, the contours of the religion were fashioned. The church itself soon became imperial, not unlike the militant empire within which it developed. In its case the authority it imposed became the more formidable in that it was aided and abetted by subscription to divine sovereignty. The church presumed to act as God's vicegerent on earth, its sovereignty thus assuming the proportions of the absoluteness of deity. This kind of societal control it maintained for as long as the human disposition continued to be that of submissiveness. In a word, the church of the Middle Ages, which had come to be by the influence of the prevailing autocracies, reigned supremely until the atmosphere in which it was immersed had been modified by the exigencies of modernity. Predictably, when the world around it was altered the church also was modified. The story of the free churches is described largely in the changes of this order which transpired.

Since this is an examination of the fortunes of a religion's history it is well to distinguish between what might be termed "sovereign ideas," on the one hand, and the horizontal sovereignties of authoritarian rule. A religion lives by the validity of its claims to "sovereign ideas," its insight into the ultimate nature of the universe. To be trustworthy a religion must communicate confidently a level of understanding of ultimate values. In a real sense, therefore, the implications of a religion's faith-perspective are absolute. They are all-inclusive. Their pertinence is both ultimate and universal. A person receives inspiration from his religion in the degree that he believes his religion speaks to him about the constituent ground of his existence. To the degree that he trusts the ultimate judgments of his faith-system, in that extent he posits in his deity the focal loyalties at the deepest levels of his being. There remain for him no value considerations which he does not define, in some fashion, in terms of the character of his God.

It is in this province of the relation between the "sovereign ideas" of a religion and its assumption of a commanding position in society which seems to constitute a severe temptation to any religious system. To qualify as a religion it must deal in what it considers to be ultimate ideas. To deal in values which it thinks are less than ultimate is to be unworthy of patronage and devotion. Yet to exist in an aura of the sense of ultimacy seems to encourage the assumption of a considerable voice in the direction of human affairs.

The medieval church during the period of the Middle Ages completely identified these two propositions. It claimed to be directly in touch with deity. And it acted in the realm of human affairs in terms of that sovereignty. The Renaissance-Reformation may be said to have begun at that point when the church with its claims of absolute sovereignty was denied the unqualified exercise of that sovereignty. The free churches were among the many by-products of this transformation.

A second element in the cultural milieu which indirectly but extensively affected the developing religious system was the almost complete absence of real knowledge of the natural world. Centuries of that development passed while the culture as a whole continued to languish in ignorance, wallowing in the doldrums of a thoroughly prescientific perspective. Prince and pauper were alike; each lived within the structures of this state of ignorance, required to pass his years chiefly guided by instinctive patterns of survival.

To be sure, the pre-Renaissance world, like its predecessors, was not lacking in curiosity about man and his life in the world. Exposure at the cutting edge of experience has a way of engendering in the human mind all kinds of questions. Man is always awed by the mysteries of his existence and his unease is proportional to the paucity of his insight. The problems of the era did not consist in any lack of interest; they were compounded of the fact that tenable answers to such questions did not exist. To that point, with but few exceptions, man's orientation had been such that he was supported with but little else than fanciful speculation about himself and his habitat.

We hasten to add that it was not an era devoid of answers to these questions which troubled the human outlook. Into the void had moved a church with an abundance of answers. Its posture of authoritarianism, growing out of its presumed rapport with deity, also yielded strong implications about knowledge. Its claims to absolute sovereignty were paralleled by its claims to an abundance of knowledge. Centuries prior to the achievement of even a modicum of understanding of the physical world the church, calling upon its reservoir of divine omniscience, confidently matched each inquiry about the operation of the physical world with what it called a "revelation." The problem of ignorance remained, however. These answers the church furnished were at best mere uneducated guesses. Basically they were false, calculated to work harm. They also served to delay indefinitely the kind of inquiry which would yield real understanding of the physical world.

This dissemination of "natural" knowledge acquired by "supernatural means" became, in a sense, a technique of the church's control over the culture. It served to intensify the passive status of the individual, discouraging human initiative and responsibility. It became an awkward predicament, an approximation of the spectacle of "the blind leading the blind." It became a prime example of medievalism at its worst, contributing to an atmosphere of the authoritarian and coersive, so formidable as to require strong incursions of modernity as a condition of any prospect of improvement.

Those strong incursions of modernity did arrive eventually. Whether the faith should have allowed itself to be bent into the shape of its surrounding, or whether the church should have refrained from speaking when it had nothing to say — these became moot questions in reckoning the religion's predicament at the beginning of the modern era. As a matter of fact the religion had become authoritarian and by its presumption of knowledge it had managed practically to isolate itself from the main stream of human experience, once Renaissance came to the Western world.

The awakening which came assumed the proportions of a groundswell. Its dynamic, fuelled by the pent-up anxieties of generations, moved the entire hemisphere in a new direction. If one were required to choose, among the myriad factors which became operative in the liberation which transpired, perhaps the discovery of what has come to be called the scientific method would be cited as a chief symptom if not the principal cause of the ferment. For more than nineteen centuries the deductive syllogisms of the Aristotelian logic had been the sole vehicle used by man in his search for knowledge. Deduction was characterized by serious limitation as far as authentic insights into nature are concerned. By it the dimensions of an entire process of investigation are contained in the premise upon which it is begun. So anxious for new knowledge was Aristotle that he appealed to what he called "first principles," mysterious flashes of insight which he thought would lead beyond one's previous experience. From these visions one deduced judgments regarding the universe.

Francis Bacon, in the sixteenth century, introduced the logical method of induction. By this method experiments are made and conclusions are drawn from the observed phenomena. Without Bacon's method what has more recently come to be known as science was impossible; with induction the burgeoning corpus of scientific knowledge became inevitable.

Employing the method, from every quarter of the civilized world men began to take nature apart, analyzing in minute detail their observations and arriving at verifiable conclusions about it. It is difficult to overestimate these tides of change which came to the West. The spirit of the age which issued from it has come to be known as the spirit of a new humanism. An entire culture came to embody the perspective expressed by Protagoras when he said that 'Man is the measure of all things.' As Lynn Harold Hough succinctly said, 'the individual man is now learning to stand in stark and lonely self-assurance, ready to defy the entire world.'

Parenthetically, it is worthy of note here that in the entire course of events from the ancient to the medieval to the modern perspective the human psyche constituted a major irony of history. Evidently, during the 'darkest night of the soul,' however heavily the weight of authoritarianism pressed upon the human outlook, at its deepest levels at least the capacity of the human mind remained fairly constant. It appears never to have been completely determined by its enviroment. Although forced by circumstance to remain dormant, at the heart of humankind there remained a fertile subsoil capable of responding to a quickening impulse. Although forced by its surroundings to relinquish its claims to a freer impulse it remained ready to spring forth in self-assertive fulfillment. That quickening impulse arrived in the recovery of an ancient humanism. From its response has come the full flowering of modernity.

The employment of the scientific method at once created for the church a real crisis. Its "revealed" insights into nature became archaic. The verifiable knowledge man now possessed stood in direct contradiction to the church's declarations about the universe. This newfound "secular" knowledge became increasingly dominant and, as a consequence, the society was artificially divided into "sacred" and "secular" compartments. In that process the church progressively was cut off from the main current of human concern. Thereafter faith was reserved for church matters and all else was consigned to the secular domain. In a word, religion became church centered rather than life centered. This underscored the church's tendency toward "otherworldliness" which under normal conditions has been a besetting inclination. For it the chief advantage of faith lay in its preparation for the "hereafter." A chief word for sin became "worldliness." Religion and science were cast into what appears to be an interminable conflict. It is fair to say that through the years since the

Renaissance religion has grudgingly withdrawn from its corpus of pseudoknowledge. However, unless it is prompted to think otherwise it is still inclined to confuse devotion with science in its approach to human need.

Like habitual patterns of individual behavior the structural forms of social institutions tend to extend themselves somewhat beyond changes in the principles and beliefs upon which they were fashioned. This tendency is noticed particularly in religious institutions which, in some instances, maintain their forms long after their belief patterns have been altered. This explains in part why in recent history a church largely medieval in form has maintained itself largely intact while operating within a cultural situation altogether different from its former habitat. An authoritarian structure once enjoyed living in a society altogether compatible with its mode of operation. That structure now addresses generations of human life being lived according to a modern perspective, among people who have come to view themselves and their world in an entirely different light.

While the main body of the medieval church has continued to be basically medieval there have occurred major alterations in many precincts of church affairs. Under the tutelage of men like Luther, Calvin, and a cadre of less conspicuous persons, all classified under the general category of Protestant Reformers, Europe and Great Britain have witnessed the establishment of churchly systems entirely apart from the prevailing churchly tradition. Even within the staid precincts of the Roman Church some modifications have occurred. Rome's motto *Roma*

Semper Eadem, became qualified by a movement from within known as the Counter Reformation. Perhaps the sole exception to the cultural modification of church life is to be found among those groups of Christians who are almost altogether otherworldly in orientation. They normally function while being practically oblivious to their earthly surroundings.

This study is designed to focus attention on that element of the Christian faith which is predicated on the assumption that the individual human being is of almost infinite worth, that he is intensely sensitive to the value structures of the universe. That in our religion which is called "the gospel" is addressed to persons thus qualified. We are of the opinion that during the early period of the religion's history that gospel did not fall on completely deaf ears but at best it can be said to have fallen largely "among thorns." By the end of its first century there had scarcely emerged from the matrix of authoritarian history a humanity qualified in disposition and circumstance to embrace that gospel without serious qualifications. Conditions were such, for centuries, that any considerable prospect for fulfillment for the humanity which lay hidden in Christianity's underlying beliefs was measurably compromised.

Eventually that qualified humanity did emerge. When it arrived, aware of its own inherent meaning, it came from deep within a developed churchly system which was inimical to man's true worth. That system did carry a considerable cargo of this "gospel" but it was burdensomely overlaid with a thick layer of worldly lore.

It is instructive to observe that here and there in Central and Northern Europe there were small groups of these qualified persons. They must have been motivated as largely by instinct as by deliberateness but they evidently felt strongly the implications of both the gospel and their qualified humanity. They promptly set about to build for themselves churches according to this different manner of thinking.

Inbibing generously of the spirit of the Renaissance, the spirit of responsible independence, these free churchmen were not guilty of bursting forth in utter defiance of all authority. But they did alter extensively the basic concept of blind acquiescence in tyrannical sovereignty, altering even an abject, passive obedience to the divine. As we shall observe in detail, revelation became for them a responsive two-party transaction. They began to embrace a concept of deity as being one who is disposed to appeal to the rational human spirit, an authority which desires to be served voluntarily and with discriminating discernment. Equipped with insights such as these they created churches which were designed to enlist the responsible participation of persons who were peculiarly respectful of God and of each other. Though negligible in size and practically overshadowed by the tides of controversy which aggravated the main bodies of the church, the free church movement deserves to be reckoned as among the most radical of the several departures which were made from the traditional Christian institution. In some respects the free churchmen proved to have possessed a clearer conception of the basic presuppositions of modernity and to have made a more consistent application, in religious thinking, of the awakened human perspective. On this account we think they deserve a more extensive acknowledgment than they have received at the hands of recent historians. This study is devoted to an examination of their posture and the premise upon which they launched their modest attempt at "doing their faith."

III

A Post-Renaissance Concept of Authority

Enough has been said to indicate that the free church movement was not an isolated event, that, instead, it emerged from deep within the cultural Renaissance and is not to be understood apart from the vast changes which the Renaissance created. This groundswell consisted in a new perspective, a different manner in which men viewed themselves and the world in which they lived. Its strength was sufficient to modify most societal structures and the few which remained relatively unchanged reflected only the strength of the tradition within which they were bound.

The free churches deserve to be described, therefore, not so much in terms of a renewal of the church as proposals to establish a new kind of religious institution, churches established upon a considerably different premise. They proposed to be new churches in an entirely new cultural situation. If in appearance they bore resemblances to traditional churches it signified only that they did propose to be churches. Their considerable common verbiage identified them as existing within the Protestant stream. In essence they deserve to be regarded as innovations in the religious community.

The free church innovation rested primarily upon the extent to which Christian disciples imbibed the Renaissance concept of authority. Prior to that time free church principles had been scarce for the same reason that principles of democratic government had been practically non-existent. Heretofore people had not thought of themselves in religion nor in government in this light; now they did think of themselves in this fashion and straightway they began to fashion institutions of both religion and government commensurate with their new ideas. Let us take a more considered account of this process.

Traditionally, religious authority has rested altogether in the "official church," i.e., in the Holy Office established and maintained on the basis of its claims to divine sanction. A corpus of "sacred literature" included the biblical materials but the Bible was not unique. It took its place among the myriad "conciliar" documents and an increasingly large body of official pronouncements, all of these writings serving to define and to elucidate the ideas of sovereignty lodged in the ecclesiastical office.

It is not an oversimplification to declare that the essential character of the entire Protestant movement is identifiable as the change which occurred as the Bible was rescued from its relatively subservient position as the supporter of church authority to a place in the thinking of all Protestant as *the citadel of authority in religion.* The main line Reformers as well as the sectarian free churchmen made the Bible the cornerstone of their approach to religion. The details of this study are concerned with whatever variations in their use of the Bible the free church-men insisted upon as compared with traditional Protestantism.

The broad contextual developments in late medieval history which made possible these changes were reviewed above. Here it is in order to examine in detail the function of the religious bodies within that reordered context, the results which flowed from the reordering of the matrix of the entire enterprise.

As has been indicated, the dawn of the modern era consisted essentially in a drastic modification of the authoritarian strictures of medievalism, strictures chiefly implemented by a practically universal empire-church, sovereignties which had been defined and enforced as being as transcendent as they were absolute. Bishop and prince alike ruled with irrefragable exactitude because the sanctions which each enjoyed were lodged in the ineffable demands of divine fiat. It is a clear indication of how powerful was the tide of humanism which ushered in the Renaissance to observe the manner and extent in which it was able to alter the concept of these sovereignties.

It will help our study to bear in mind, as we assess the changes which did occur, that central to the legacy which came to the church from its medieval background were two seminal concepts, each of which, in turn, was to pose a real problem for religion in a modernized circumstance. The first of these ideas was the idea of God which came to it practically intact from medievalism. It was an idea whose marks of Hebrew antiquity had been reinforced by all that Augustine's Neo-Platonism could bring to it, an idea, incidentally, which from that period to the present has remained largely unchanged. Again, there was a multi-storied cosmology, a model of the universe whose frame dated from ancient Greece, whose outlines were sufficiently substantial to have withstood the erosive effects of Aristotle's para-evolutionary science and to have been maintained for a period of more than eighteen hundred years as the design upon which pagan and Christian alike were obliged to hang their entire outlook. It was abandoned as a working concept of the world by the natural sciences as a prime consequence of the Copernican Revolution but, as in the case of the concept of God, for the popular mind, including the vast majority of religious thinking, it has persistently constituted the central assumption. Since cosmology is basic to vocabulary in any province of experience, it follows that any considerable modification of a world-model eventually issues in a reinvestment of language symbols. The world of science has pursued its course with relative freedom to talk in terms of a different world order; it is an operation in which religion, in general, has been much more reluctant to engage.

As a matter of course, for broad areas of man's experience medievalism's absolutes did give way to what may be termed a "modern relativism." Individualism has increasingly characterized its perspective. The familiar lines of political and economic development, for example, are evidence of the gradual but definite redefinition which has been the result of the change.

At this point it is fair to insist that, although it was being acted upon by the same forces as those affecting the political and economic structures, there did remain for religion a problem of much graver order. As indicated, unlike these other provinces, the moorings of religion were much more securely anchored in the past. Notwithstanding the difficulties which they, too, encountered, these other provinces, with relative ease, moved to divorce themselves from their traditional absolutes and, in regard to their value structures, pragmatically achieved a measure of independence. Religion, on the other hand, found it necessary to affect changes within limits imposed upon it by loyalties to factors which did not lend themselves to alteration. In politics, for example, if an emperor impeded the path of progress he could be beheaded. Any appreciable change in the status of deity required a less drastic resort.

In a word, religion faced the problem of altering the functional operation of its faith while preserving intact the traditional deference for the eternal. It had to make changes in its technique of authority with little changes in its concept of deity. It must find room for a rapidly accelerating awareness of the freedom and responsibility of man while retaining inviolate its reverence for God whose "wholly otherness" was removed from all that is mundane by all that a "holy supernaturalism" could define.

Parenthetically, it might serve to qualify the emotional preference of contemporary Christian minds for the term, "supernatural" if they should become aware that the term was one devised by Aristotle to describe, critically, what he took to be Plato's concept of nature. He accused Plato of superimposing upon nature what Aristotle called a supernature. Aristotle had no way of anticipating that his contrived vocabulary would eventually receive Christian baptism.

In retrospect, what were the options which were open to the sixteenth century Christian mind with regard to authority?

On the one hand, for the majority there could be maintained loyalty to the *status quo*, deriving at least a modicum of excitement, if it were so disposed, from the slight variations which were being made upon authoritarianism by the pressures of the Renaissance. A second option was opened by Luther and Calvin who focused the entire matter in the Bible instead of in the church, thereby acquiring the advantage of a fixed seat of authority while surrendering none of that authority's transcendence and, with proper indulgence in the biblical verbiage, it could gratify both its devotional and its rational needs, provided, of course, it embraced Luther and Calvin in that order.

As a third option it could choose a position which was consonant with the premise as well as the spirit of the Renaissance by injecting into the entire pattern of faith-value a factor which we have referred to above by the term, a "new humanism." This option provided for a considerable reduction in the element of transcendence and its concept of authority was proportionately less absolute and more relative. This was due to the fact that it was predicated on a two-party revelatory transaction, one in which man himself is required to become a sensitive, responsible participant. We are of the opinion that the free churchmen attempted to exercise this third option.

It is well to bear in mind that the position which the free churchmen fostered arose from within that held by the Protestants generally. As part of the Reformation they, too, had shifted from the church to the Bible as the touchstone of authority. It should be added that there is implicit in this overall position of the Reformers at least an indication of the direction the Radicals would eventually take when their dissatisfactions had persuaded them that they should also divorce themselves from the larger Protestant movement.

In this regard, aside, I am not disposed to overlook the suggestion which is sometimes made to the effect that geography and ethnology contributed extensively to the Reformation. Those of this persuasion insist that the Reformation may have had its inception when Christianity moved from the confines of the Mediterranian basin to include the Germanic people of central and northern Europe. It may be that there is more significance to "blood and soil" than we sometimes think. Perhaps it was no mere happenstance that a religion which could occupy itself so extensively with its dogmatic preciseness and its ecclesiastical efficiency so long as it numbered among its followers principally citizens of Graeco-Roman extraction, should burst forth in concern for such things as "justification by faith only," once it had come to include a generous portion of the warm-blooded Teutons in its ranks. There are, indeed, impressive parallels in the ethnic and doctrinal developments which occurred.

Be that as it may, it was this human factor, the element which had furnished the real point of departure for the Reformers, which also became the issue which separated the free churchmen from the Reformers. They became "radical" in their concept of man, going far beyond anything which had been proposed, or even permitted, by Luther and Calvin, the concept which, likewise, identified them as being much truer disciples of the Renaissance.

This insistence upon a larger human responsibility issued at once in a sharp difference over the status of the Bible as the "Word of God," modifying conspicuously the role of the interpreter in any meaningful appropriation of its message.

As we make comparisons in regard to matters like these we must not forget that all the thinking of all the parties was done at a time prior to the advent of the modern historical-critical method of biblical study. Clear distinctions are a bit more difficult to come by, therefore, and, in most instances, for an evaluation of positions being entertained, one is left largely to identifying them by observing their long-range development. However, at the time the differences of which we now speak arose and became strong enough to become divisive. Their peculiar characteristics did become increasingly distinct with the passing of time.

As to the source of the Bible's inspiration, always a clue to the character of the authority ascribed to it, — in fact, always the exact correlative of the claims made for its authority — Protestantism rested its case on the assumption that "God is its author".

For example, in several instances language to this effect is found in Calvin's *Institutes*. The work as a whole is so imbued with Augustine's notions of the absolute sovereignty of God that, had it not contained repeated references to the Scriptures as 'words from the mouth of God,' one could scarcely avoid the conclusion that Calvin subscribed to some kind of "dictation" theory of inspiration. However, his language in early sections of the work leave nothing to conjecture.

> . . . We establish it with a certainty superior to human judgment (just as if we actually beheld the presence of God Himself in it) that Scripture came to us, by the ministry of men, from the very mouth of God.
>
> (*Institutes*, I. 7, 4f.)

(Other references from the *Institutes* elaborating on Calvin's notion of divine authorship of the Bible:

> But since we are not favored by daily oracles from heaven, and since it is only in the Scriptures that the Lord has been pleased to preserve his truth in personal remembrance, it obtains the same complete credit and authority with believers, when they are satisfied of its divine origin, as if they heard the very words pronounced by God himself.
>
> I. 7, 1.

> Therefore being illumined by him, we now believe the divine origin of the Scriptures, not from our own judgment or that of others, but we esteem the certainty, that we received it from God's own mouth by the ministry of men, to be superior to any human judgment, and equal to that of an intuitive perception of God himself in it.
>
> I. 7, 5.

> Herein God designs to confer a singular privilege on his elect, whom he distinguishes from the rest of mankind. For what is the beginning of the true learning but a prompt alacrity to hear the voice of God.
>
> I. 7, 4.

> It must be maintained . . . that we are not established in the belief of the doctrine till we are indubitably persuaded that God is its author.
>
> I. 7, 4.

(John Calvin, *Institutes of the Christian Religion*, John Allen, Jr. Seventh American edition, Revised

and corrected by Benjamin B. Warfield. Philadelphia: Presbyterian Board of Christian Education, 1936, pp. 85ff.)

In fairness it should be added that on purely logical grounds Calvin argued for man's right to interpret the Scripture and opened the way for what might have become exciting levels of human insight by his appeal to what he called the "inner witness of the Spirit" to vouchsafe the authentic meaning of the word. It is to be regretted that this notion, too, was encapsulated within the narrow confines of his authoritarian conclusions.

Luther, with amazing venturesomeness, established an empirical basis for determining that the Bible is the true Word of God, even daring to risk the application of the principle to particular portions of the Bible, witness his estimate of the Epistle of James. However, he soon became obsessed with opinions which he himself had arrived at by the exercise of his own resources and spent the remainder of his life contending against those who, by the exercise of these same prerogatives, differed with his interpretation.

Thus, in the case of both Luther and Calvin, their acts nullified any overtures in the direction of the principle of private interpretation which may have been implied in their recovery of the Bible as authoritative. In a word, because Luther became so devoutly gratified, and because Calvin considered himself to be so correct, the image of each contradicted the spirit of individualism out of which they both had sprung. Hence, from where they stood it was but an easy step to the rigid, sterile precincts of Protestant Scholasticism into which the multitudes of each succeeding generation have been plunged. That Scholasticism's authoritarian strategem was not wasted on the Catholics, whose taunting rejoinder accurately labelled it: "You have merely substituted an infallible book for an infallible church."

In this connection I am not averse to the notion that, notwithstanding the overwhelming proportions of change which characterized the transition to the modern world, strong traces of medievalism also continued to be at work. For example, it is a matter of record that the recovery of Aristotle's metaphysical theories produced in Aquinas a "nature-Synthesis" which served to dull somewhat the edge of absolutism for Catholics. The recovery of the classics also became the occasion, in general, of the rise of the New Learning. Nevertheless, there remained intact Aristotle's logic, which for so long had been practiced almost universally.

As was indicated above, that logic was predicated upon the idea that certain First Principles, axiom-like truisms of thought, are available to the human reason. These are said to be impressed upon the human mind by Reality and require no proof of their validity. Given these self-evident First Principles, deductive logicians practiced their art with mathematical preciseness, their conclusions being safe-guarded by rules of truth and fallacy which were also prescribed by Aristotle.

This deductive logic is the exact pattern of the thinking of those, then and now, who claim "verbal inspiration" as the only source, and exegetical interpretation as the sole technique for arriving at what some describe as "the naked word of God." The parallel is so strong it is difficult to believe that it is merely coincidental that this Scholastic biblicism arose in the wake of the recovery of biblical authority, unaffected by an intellectual climate which was habitually given to this type of logical exercise.

It is not mere deference tempered with charity to acknowledge that the Protestant leaders were so engrossed in a project of watershed proportions, namely, that of identifying a locus of dependable revelatory significance with which to replace the vagaries of historical churchly authority, that they became practically oblivious to what impression their methods would make upon their successors. Their project as a whole was shot through with the aura of modernity and, given the intensity of the contest, perhaps they are to be forgiven for the tone of absoluteness with which they argued their case. It is to be lamented, however, that the majority of their followers were primarily persuaded by these narrower insinuations of their pronouncements rather than by the full implications of their Protestant posture.

It was at the point where the majority lost its nerve and reverted to the security of authoritarian biblicism that the free churchmen became offended and struck out in a direction other than that of the main body of the Reformation. We repeat, that was the point, also, where the Protestors against the Protestants disclosed that they were truer sons of the Renaissance.

It is to their greater credit to recall that they, too, did not have access to critical knowledge of the production and interpretation of the Bible. Perhaps their acts were motivated more largely by instinct than from insight, therefore, but in any event, they broke away from the New Scholasticism and, predictably, for that break they paid the usual price. They had to exercise a rare patience to await the results of their position, results which only centuries afterward are becoming increasingly obvious.

These sectarians were radical in their contention that *within the human psyche the revelatory work of God is continually creative.* More recently, this item in them is sometimes referred to as their conception of "the effective presence of the Holy Spirit." In the writings of men like Hendry and Van Dusen are to be found references of this order. For example, in his *The Holy Spirit in Christian Theology*, Hendry claims that in the case of the main line Reformers there was no appreciation of this idea. In them the Spirit was appealed to solely as agent for the efficacy of the Scriptures upon man and, he goes on to say, "the theology of the Reformation . . . implies the virtual elimination of the human spirit as a factor in man's encounter with the gospel." (George S. Hendry, *The Holy Spirit in Christian Theology.* Philadelphia: The Westminster Press, 1956, p. 101.)

Van Dusen introduced his remarks on the subject with this statement:

> It was left to the despised Anabaptists to claim that the inward voice of the Holy Spirit takes precedence over the external word of the Scriptures, or the dictates of prelates.

He continues, making the point emphatically:

> The distinctive contention of Radical or Sectarian Protestantism with respect to the Holy Spirit is two fold:
>
> 1.   That the leading of the Holy Spirit is not confined to the confirmation of the word of Scripture, but guides into "new truth" which God desires to reveal to his children in special and novel circumstances of their contemporary life.

> 2. That the operation of the Holy Spirit is not limited to the channels of officials of the institutional church, but comes directly to expectant and contrite spirits in our time as it has through the ages.

He then proceeds to summarize this distinction thus:

> The issue between Catholicism or Classic Protestantism, on the one hand, and Radical Protestantism, on the other, is, largely, the issue between *Tradition* and *Creativity* . . .
>
> In more familiar and significantly religious terms, the issue is between the "priestly" and the "prophetic."

(Henry P. Van Dusen, *Spirit, Son and Father.* New York: Charles Scribner's Sons, 1958, pp. 82, 136f, 144.)

Bear in mind that both Hendry and Van Dusen were writing from within Classic Protestantism.

From the point of view of Free Churchmen, Daniel Jenkins, in a work entitled *Tradition, Freedom, and the Spirit,* elaborates this distinction by naming effects for vital religion of its excessive indulgence in what he calls the merely traditional.

> . . . . Christians, with the experience behind them of the calling and rejection of the Old Israel and out of that rejection the birth of the New, should be in a position to learn from tradition without being misled by it. . . . the Church, throughout her history, has shown a curious awareness of those dangers (of the traditional) and much error and corruption have come into her life through a misreading of her past. . . . Tradition has not fulfilled its proper function of lighting up her knowledge of God and His ways with His people, but has ministered only to destructive self-righteousness and pride.
>
> At least three dangers appear to be inherent in the attitude of the church toward tradition. These are present even when tradition is appealed to in the most careful and responsible way unless they are balanced by an equally

powerful realization of the Spirit in the midst of the here and now, and of the necessity of making new decisions in faith.

The first danger is that of formalism. When appeal becomes not one side of the dialectical movement of the man of faith trying to reach a decision but an act complete in itself, this danger is bound to arise. The light of God's truth is not sought as that which appeared in a particular situation in the past, which must be brought in as one relevant factor among others in a new and different situation, but the intellectual residue of the old is forced into the mould of the new without sufficient attention being paid to what is distinctive in either.

The second danger is . . . legalism (which) may, perhaps, be described as the ethical expression of formalism. Because the power of free decision under the guidance of the Spirit is underestimated, the relevance of principles of conduct formulated to meet past situations is exaggerated and excessive weight is given to the authority of precedent. Legalism is always disposed to depreciate the element of novelty in a situation and to meet its challenge by acting in accordance with a habit of disciplined conduct, which does not necessarily involve personal commitment.

A third danger is archaism . . . (which) is the invariable fruit of legalism. Because the criteria which it has learned to apply were formulated in a past age and no longer perfectly apply in the present, traditionalism looks wistfully to a time in the past when its criteria were applicable and its specific for the ills of the present is a restoration of this idealized past. The result is that instead of living 'between the times,' the Church contrives only to 'live behind the times.' Her spokesmen spend their days lamenting as ills what may only be innovations, and instead of striving to shape the direction of a vigorous and rapidly moving world, they content themselves with trying as far as possible to pretend that the world is not there.

(Daniel Jenkins, *Tradition, Freedom and the Spirit.* Philadelphia: The Westminster Press, 1951, pp. 114f)

This extensive excerpt from Jenkins indicates that Jenkins thinks that the free churchmen had come to believe what the church generally had overlooked, namely, that to know the fullness of New Life one must go considerably beyond the mere verbiage of the church's first century documents by participating in the insights acquired through contemporary levels of spiritual experience.

We have quoted extensively from these authors because their statements describe for us what I think the free churchmen had in mind. Our early forebears would have been impressed with expressions which we have come to use. For example, expressions such as "The Bible is the record of revelation" would have pleased them. They anticipated much of what historical-critical insights have subsequently yielded by insisting on putting biblical accounts alongside contemporary divine-human encounters. They appear to have sensed that, included in the extensive biblical chronology is an almost infinite variety of experience, varied in intensity as well as in circumstance. It spoke to them of persons under many conditions, responsibly relating what it means to be 'overtaken by the eternal,' a kind of experience which is both identifiable and consequential, then and now. The Bible was for these sectarians, therefore, *a true example of religious experience*, faithfully revealing that for many of the characters represented in it that experience was rewardingly adequate; for others it proved to be woefully weak, with discernable reasons for each. They sensed also that there is not a great deal of satisfaction to be derived solely from familiarity with this record of ancient involvement, however respectful one may become of the conditions under review, nor was that involvement to be reproduced merely by acquaintance with the Bible's detailed description. They proposed, instead, that a faith-experience satisfactory for any succeeding generation must be achieved solely by a then rapport with the God who had thus demonstrated in the biblical witness his ways with men. In a word, faith-experience, they insisted, must be existential, not merely recitative of the experience of others recorded from the ancient past. They believed that is not enough for contemporary persons merely to know what God meant to Peter, James and John.

Thinking on this order is to be deemed "radical" only in the context of the sordid monotony of a purely traditional and authoritarian situation. Against that kind of background it does appear to be conspicuously "radical."

It is obvious from the above discussion that these remarks are addressed to the principles which the free churchmen espoused; it is not a discussion of how the vast majority of more recent groups who claim to be their heirs have practiced these ideas. It is to be lamented that any treatment of the practice of most recent free churches would be awkwardly brief. Most contemporary free churchmen seek to resolve all issues, great and small, by the easy affirmation which begins: "The Bible speaks of it . . ."

They, too, compromise vital religion by seeking smug security in the notion that revelation is strictly a one-party transaction, constituted as a completely transcendent sovereignty by the express will of the Almighty, and designed to press its mandate upon a passive humanity by acting always as a factor coercively external to human responsibility.

This popular appeal to biblical verbiage is impressive because normally there is present sufficient

reluctance in the human spirit to offset any level of
maturity which may be inclined to exercise a weight-
ier way. A two-party concept of revelation does
require a substantial measure of maturity in those
who venture to employ it but it also has its rewards.
It is calculated to engender in those who pursue it a
remarkable level of strength. It entails, as well, the
calculated risk that those who would employ it
become careless and irresponsibly dogmatic in their
responses. In this respect the principle is peculiarly
paradoxical. It is a principle which deserves to be
judged on the basis of its inherent worth, however,
rather than by any or all of the extravaganzas of
misuse to which it has been put and to which it is
obviously vulnerable. Much more must be said about
this principle.

There is merit in the suggestion that it is for the
lack of the responsible exercise of this mature principle that the charge of irrelevancy is lodged against
much of religious thought in the modern world. It
may be that what we often take to be an attitude of
indifference on the part of the gain-saying world is,
instead, the modern mind's impatience with contemporary religion's archaic traditionalism.

As a matter of fact, this basic difference between
what Van Dusen calls the "priestly" and the "prophetic" is reflected, even, in the symbolism of our faith-
perspective. For the most part theological literature
is couched in language which is meaningful strictly
within an ecclesiastical context. Only a relatively
small part of it has ventured to transpose faith's
basic concepts into symbols which are life-oriented
and, we regret to add, for these few theologians we

have continued to reserve, at best, a marginal status within the cult.

We are encouraged to think, generally, if trends are to be trusted, that a more creative concept of authority will become increasingly evident in the years immediately ahead. For example, much of the Roman Catholic world is insisting on major alterations in its traditionally authoritarian structure. Also, with apparent ease a great deal of the Protestant world respectfully relegated the Neo-Calvinism of Karl Barth to a prominent place in its museum. In some respects this eclipse of Barth's theological system occurred some years prior to his own demise. There is encouragement to think that what John Baillie called "low religion," with its premium on the *external and the abnormal*, is largely *passé*, that, instead, the modern mind yearns for the substantially gratifying dimensions of "high religion" with its premium on the *internal* and the *normal* in human experience. This shift in emphasis lends encouragement in the direction of the free church enterprise.

IV

The Church and Its Members

The church that Littell described as "a community of disciples" is defined more in detail in an observation made by a British free churchman:

> Our young friend thought he was "joining" the church; he may awake to the much more serious discovery that he is helping to "constitute" it — that the church . . . is not a hierarchy of officials, with an appendage of laymen, but a society of men and women drawn together by common convictions and needs, and entering into a social experience of the Christian faith for which their individual experience has so far prepared them.

(H. Wheeler Robinson, *The Life and Faith of Baptists.* London: Methuen, 1927, p. 99.)

The implications of statements like these serve to underscore the radical departure from traditional ecclesiology which the free churchmen made. For centuries past the church had lived by an ancient rule: "Outside the church there is no salvation." It had long since come to be acknowledged as being the vicegerent of God on the earth. It had become a formidable institutional structure into which persons were inducted so as to receive the benefits of a salvation which the church alone was qualified to administer.

It was now being proposed that the dynamics of a satisfactory religious experience are not centered in the church but, instead, *are centered in human life.* Each person is endowed with capacities which make him competent to meet all the demands with which genuine religion confronts him. These free churchmen assumed that divine grace addresses itself to persons *where they are*, within the ebb and flow of their actual life situation.

". . . a Christian needs no priest in addition to Christ as mediator in the innermost center of the temple, with God himself. For in the last resort he has been given an immediate access to God which no ecclesiastical authority can disturb, still less take away from him," this the affirmation of Hans Küng. (*On Being a Christian.* [Garden City, New York: Doubleday, 1976], p. 481.)

These free churchmen thought of themselves as having become disciples while outside the church. They had become bold to declare, on the basis of their own experience: "Outside the church there *is* salvation." The church may be, and often is, the chief means of inspiring a person's impressions of the divine presence. It does not follow, however, that God in the awareness of the individual is so closely associated with the church as to justify equating the church and the processes of revelation. The church may serve to define and to bring into focus the awareness of the God factor in human consciousness. When the "moment of truth" arrives, however, there is described a circle in which only two may stand, namely, God and the individual human being.

The rise of this movement is the more remarkable, given the fact that it arose among sixteenth century people who were, in the main, a peasant folk. They had little access to historical resources, except the biblical materials, with which to make comparative analysis of the ecclesiastical alternatives to the problems they felt obliged to address. It is for this reason we think their motives were couched principally in the Renaissance perspective. They were immersed in the emerging awareness of human resources and responsibilities and, encouraged by that awareness, they approached the teachings of the Bible, making a deliberate redefinition of religious faith.

The redefining they did was predicated on impressive *minimal levels of maturity* in those who would become members of their congregations. These minimal requirements became an index of their polity of *adult membership* and were reflected in the ramifications of their churchmanship. Persons were considered as qualified candidates for belonging to the church who were old enough to deal with matters of spiritual concern, sufficiently mature to engage responsibly in the affairs of church life.

It was on this basis that they rejected the traditional practice of what they called "pedo-baptism," the almost universal practice of administering initiatory rites to infants. Like the Reformers, they subscribed to the principle of "Justification by faith only" as the basis of church membership. Unlike the Reformers, the free churchmen insisted that persons should, themselves, exercise that faith. Their contention was that if a person is capable of exercising faith-experience he is obligated to do so. They made no provision in their thinking for a person sponsoring or representing another in matters religious. They made no provision for *proxy religion.*

Like their neighbors, the Reformers, they appealed not to the regimen of medievalism, but to the Bible as the touchstone of their perspective. However, the use that they and the Reformers made of the book served to cast the Bible itself into a considerably different status. As indicated above, for centuries the church had grouped the book together with others of its "traditions," consisting largely in what it had preserved of the authoritative teachings of its hierarchy. The Reformers and the free churchmen managed to break through the several layers of denigration to which it had been subjected, restoring it to a singular place of authority. The judgments which they derived from its use are the more remarkable in that for them its verbiage stood practically alone. It was not until much more recently that there was acquired any appreciable insight into the historical character of its literature.

In their use of the Bible they did enjoy two distinct advantages. They were able to exercise a privilege which they reserved for themselves, namely, the right to interpret the book for themselves. And they were prepared to make these interpretations in the light of their new focus on human initiative and responsibility. Obviously the book yielded for them a far richer significance than they had known within the traditional church. From its use they fashioned a radical break with traditional ecclesiology. It is fair to say that it remained for their more recent lineal heirs to rationalize what they had done.

This early propensity for a biblical foundation the movement has rather consistently maintained. Here it should be emphasized that at no point in a free church enterprise is the requisite of a minimal maturity more conspicuously exemplified than in its use of the biblical materials. This becomes particularly evident in its exercise of its cornerstone principle of private interpretation.

A pervasive immaturity is now apparent among free churches. There are many who fail to distinguish between the high privilege of interpreting the book for themselves, on the one hand, and, on the other, the responsibility of trying to determine what its authors intended it to mean. When one fails to make this distinction he is victimized by a besetting fallacy, namely, the idea that *the Bible must be taken to mean what it means to me.* It goes without saying that the meaning of the Bible *for an individual* at any given time does consist in nothing more or less than what that person has determined its meaning to be.

It should be admitted, parenthetically, that a respectful deference which a person has for the book, like his deference for things sacred in general, does appear at times to issue in an element of reverence in his life which is greater than the sum of all the parts of his actual knowledge of it would seem to warrant. It does not follow, however, that the book's meaning is limited to a person's understanding of it at any given time.

It is difficult to overestimate the possibilities inherent in this principle of private interpretation, possibilities both for chaotic confusion and for the strength of an incisive concensus which may flow from its use. For the prospects of the confusion which the abuse of the principle may create, witness the sectarian dismemberment of the Christian world which has occurred in recent history. On the other hand, to weigh the advantages which may be acquired by employing the principle of private interpretation, consider the dynamics of the togetherness of a host of people, qualified by maturity, devoutly engaged upon Christian mission. From its abuse much life has been sacrificed upon the altar of confusion. Far too little effort has been focused upon its legitimate employment.

It is interesting to observe the exasperation which sometimes follows upon its abuse, the radical resorts which are invoked so as to avoid such consequences. These result in frequent forays into appeals for "authoritative," canonical interpretations, desperate attempts to bring order out of the chaos. On the other hand, in order to achieve a semblance of concensus techniques of simplistic instruction are a favorite resort, attempts at reducing biblical meaning to the least common denominator. The implications of a straightforward, thoroughgoing use of the principle of private interpretation are seldom taken seriously into account.

For any congregation that would take seriously its biblical moorings the matter of trying to maintain a minimum level of maturity adequate to preserve a tenable biblical interpretation poses a real problem. As has been indicated, it involves a great deal more than the mere assumption of the basic principle of private interpretation. It requires a level of insight upon which an ecclesiology of the free church order can be erected. Since there is usually present a considerable tendency toward popularization, a perspective which encourages believing in the *obvious* meaning of the Bible, there is usually present a pressure toward a simplistic idea of revelation.

Those who insist on the obvious meaning of scripture usually assume that "the word of God" was given by divine fiat, that every facet of the divine will may, therefore be discerned by reference to an appropriate part of the Bible. To those who think this is true the book must be "inerrant"; it becomes a "rule book" which, if neatly indexed, conveniently yields a divine answer to any problem which may arise in human experience.

On the analogy of mathematics, trying to interpret all biblical material on the level of the literalist is like insisting that in the resolution of all mathematical problems only the simple processes of addition and subtraction are to be employed. To admit that there are problems sufficiently complex as to require more complex processes, such as, for example, the Binomial Theorem, for their resolution, it does not follow that the processes of addition and subtraction are "untrue."

The free churchmen employed a much more complex approach to biblical interpretation, one which required a more mature level of insight than that of the literalist. The conclusions they arrived at were not mere copy-book recitations of biblical verbiage. As they viewed the matter, ecclesiology was not based primarily on what the Bible had to say about the church but on its teachings regarding the preparation of persons who would be so disposed toward each other as to be interested in forming a church. To fashion a church on precisely what the Bible taught about church would run the risk, they thought, of missing the free church outlook altogether. They considered the literal use of the biblical language to be the primary source of a legalistically authoritarian institution against which they sought to erect a different kind of structure.

The strong inferences in the Bible about man, his condition and his redemption they considered to be primary. Admittedly, this method serves to reduce greatly the traditional emphasis on the church, but this they welcomed also. For them the church is important but its importance is relative. It deserves to be placed farther down in the scale of priorities. It should take its place as an accompanying circumstance, a chief consequence of the basic concepts of revelation and redemption.

It is difficult to reconcile this free church outlook with those who insist on literalism. As was indicated in the discussion of biblical authority, above, free churchmen view revelation as being a two-party transaction. They accept the pages of the Bible as the by-product of the experience of persons in real life situations, persons who, in those situations, encountered the overtures of divine grace. Moreover, they are prepared to understand that all such encounters as the authors of the book knew reflect the conditions under which these encounters occurred. They take this to mean, therefore, that all encounters were not on the same level of intensity and import. From this they understand that parts of the biblical record carry much larger cargoes of divine revelation than do other accounts. Believing that the Bible was created in this manner, they assume that biblical interpretation consists essentially in the obverse of the process in which it was created. One is supposed to determine its meaning in the extent that he carefully reconstructs the conditions under which it was recorded.

Since revelatory experience is a two-party trans-action, consisting essentially in a relationship be-tween persons, most free churchmen are enthusiastic about those qualities which are said to be peculiar to personal knowledge, qualities like those proposed by Martin Buber in a work entitled, *I and Thou*. (Martin Buber, *I and Thou*. Edinburgh: T. and T. Clark, 1937, Ronald Gregory Smith, Jr.)

Buber contends that in the knowing experience persons are related to each other on a plane distinct from that which characterizes the relation between a person and a thing. In scientific knowledge, for example, a person addresses an object of knowledge as an *it*. The person knows the object but is not known by the object. On the other hand, a primary ingredient of personal knowledge is its reciprocity. Whatever else I may know about another person, primarily I am aware that that person also knows me. In knowing persons as persons we become un-avoidably involved in a relationship with those per-sons. Buber's lament is that in far too many instances, particularly in a culture which is largely scientific in orientation, persons are inclined to address other persons as if they were nothing more than things. When this occurs, he says, the relationship which is peculiar to personal knowledge is destroyed.

Buber's idea about personal knowledge and per-sonal involvement is not unlike the concept of "ultimacy" in Paul Tillich's concept of worship. When one worships the divine, a deity characterized by "ultimacy," according to Tillich, it is a positive, creative experience. On the other hand, when a person bestows worship on that which is less than worthy of worship, it becomes for the worshipper a demonic, destructive experience.

Distinctions such as these become the more apparent when the specific biblical foundations of ecclesiology are examined.

Parenthetically, it is well to note that in any review of biblical language in justification of an existing type of church order it is well to bear in mind that each of the three chief types of ecclesiology which have been employed by the religion has been fairly successful in justifying its practice by appeal to the Bible. Advocates of the episcopal, the presbyterial or representative, and those who favor congregational democracy — each of these has found evidence of support in biblical usage. This would seem to indicate that there are factors other than strictly linguistic considerations which may have influenced thinking about matters of church.

To establish a biblical foundation for the church many free churchmen do not point to specific references in which the church is discussed by the biblical writers. Instead, they point to New Testament language which reflects rather indirectly the character and purpose of the early church situation. In contrast to those who seek the legitimacy of the institution in a specific act of Jesus in constituting the church, persons of this persuasion are impressed with how casually Jesus appears to have approached the grouping of his disciples. His earliest references depict him as being willing to concentrate on the kind of disposition his impressions on them produced, apparently confident that their association in group experience, their church life, as we have come to call it, would follow as a matter of course. Given his confidence in the transformation which their discipleship affected, he evidenced no unease regarding whether they would become associated with each other.

There is the implication in Littell's use of the term, "a community of disciples," that sixteenth century free churchmen thought of the church as coming into being incidental to Jesus' ministry. The focus is on discipleship. Jesus' concern, they thought, was in them becoming his disciples, that if they did he expected an aggregation to be the normal outgrowth of their rapport with him. With Jesus the early disciples participated in a revelatory experience. Gradually they came to an understanding of him and out of that relationship there came to be a "Jesus crowd."

After he had associated with them for several months, while on a holiday occasion, he inquired as to the level of their insight into the nature of his ministry. He appears to be enthusiastic about what they professed. "Others have their *ekklesia*," he exclaimed, "but *my* kind of crowd will be composed of people who are thus qualified." What they had come to know in him would become the magnetic principle fashioning their "togetherness."

As a matter of fact, this casualness in Jesus of which we speak is echoed in his use of the common noun, *ekklesia*, a compound term which did eventually come to be used with reference to Christian bodies. Contrary to the sometimes expressed notion when Jesus used this term, Matthew 16:16-18, he was making specific reference to an act in which he instituted the church, there is substance to the idea that at that point in his ministry with his disciples he was making no reference to the institutional church.

The word, *ekklesia* had had a long history of common usage. It was a compound term, composed of two words, *ek* and *kaleo*, meaning literally, "called out." It was used to refer to any aggregation of persons whose "togetherness" was the result of being gathered around a common purpose or cause. Its particular connotation was always derived from its modifying circumstance. In this respect its meaning was an approximation of what in English is expressed by the word, crowd. It sometimes referred to an unruly *ekklesia*, a mob. It often designated an assembly for the purpose of civil government. As a matter of fact, the New Testament writers used the term in these as well as in other senses. It was much later that it came to designate Christian groups, at a time when there had come to be such groups to be thus designated. Even so, its usage in religious circles continued to parallel precisely its general usage. It remained for centuries of development to give it the weight of a proper noun reference implicit in our term, church.

So universal had become the tradition of a legalistic, authoritarian institution, this concept of the church among the sixteenth century free churchmen was at once a conspicuous innovation. More recently, the idea has become less exceptional. It is now being expressed in many quarters, even among those whose affinities have been most traditional. For example, Hans Küng, a Roman Catholic theologian, is unequivocal in his affirmation:

> The church might be briefly defined as the community of those who believe in Christ. More precisely: not founded by Jesus, but emerging after his death in his name as crucified and yet living, *the community of those who have become involved in the cause of Jesus Christ and who witness to it as hope for all men.* (Küng's italics.)

(Hans Küng, *On Being a Christian*, p. 478.)

Notwithstanding the fact that occasionally one hears an expression such as Küng's from those who normally subscribe to a strictly legalistic inauguration of the Christian institution, it is with grave difficulty that many who profess to be free churchmen are able to avoid a legalistic account of the church's origin. For example, a nineteenth century free churchman, whose ideas have been widely influential in free church circles, made this disposition of the problem:

> This organization, called here "kingdom" and "church," is the conception of the divine mind, the expression of the divine thought, and the embodiment of the divine authority on earth. . . . They were used as synonymous terms by the evangelists so long as Christ has but *one* organization for they were one and the same body. So soon as the "churches were multiplied" a distinction arose. The kingdom embraced the first church, and it now embraced all the churches. The churches of Christ constitute the kingdom of Christ . . . as all the separate sovereign States of these United States constitute the Republic of America. Now, as no foreigner can become a citizen of this Republic without being naturalized as a citizen of some one of the States, no one can enter the kingdom of Christ without becoming a member of some one of his visible churches.

(James R. Graves, *Old Landmarkism, What is it?* Texarkana, Arkansas-Texas: Baptist Sunday School Committee, 1928, pp. 29, 33.)

Relying on claims of unbroken succession from the first century origins of the church, the successionalists take great pride in being what they call a "New Testament church." Many free churchmen also make this designation but they evidence no sympathy with a successional basis for the claim. They think of their church as being biblical in the sense that it, also, emerged within the conditions of "discipleship," an approximation of the conditions under which the first century congregations emerged.

After the passing of centuries of Western history, a history replete with the presumptions of an authoritarian institution *administering* Christian faith, conditions had become such that resourceful persons could acquire, voluntarily, a faith-orientation and, acting in the same sense of responsible personhood, they were free to commit themselves to each other in the "togetherness" of Christian groups. Bound to each other by their mutual loyalties, they devoted themselves, as groups, to worship and service, comparable to the disposition and activity of the earliest congregations. In this sense they think it is appropriate to call themselves "New Testament" churches.

In the routine process of conducting "church business" free church congregations function according to the democratic principles implicit in their constitution. Their decisions are agreed upon by any proportionate method they may choose to employ. Perhaps, in usual circumstances, a majority opinion of the group determines its choice.

The group action regarding the addition of members is usually considered to be an exceptional issue. An adult seeking union with an aggregation of adults entails a completely mutual assent. The person seeking membership is impressly favorably with the spiritual perspective, the "discipleship" of the congregation. The "body of believers" is, in turn, aggreably impressed with the qualifications of the one seeking membership. Their mutual acceptance forges the bond of their union. Anything less than complete agreement will prove to be divisively damaging to the body as a whole.

If in considering a request for membership there are those in the congregation who object to approving the request, that objection and the application itself both deserve to be considered on precisely the same level, namely, on the basis of *discipleship*. To consider a request or an objection to its approval on any other ground places in jeopardy the church's qualification as a Christian congregation. Its membership, which is its constituent ingredient, would become secondary to peripheral concerns.

If in contradiction to the objection a request for membership is approved on the basis of a mere majority there is created at the heart of the group itself, *ipso facto,* a rift destructive of the church's constitution. Solely on the basis of mathematical logic, if one is added and by the addition another is deprived of the fellowship, no addition has been made by the process. By the decision a breach has been made in the "togetherness" which is the *sine qua non* of the church's existence.

In principle free churchism furnishes a fresh departure in religious orientation. It is focused, not upon corporate aggrandizement, but upon the cultivation of the individual person at the centers of his character-motivational structure. A church's constitution rests squarely upon a consistent implementation of the dimensions of an inspired and responsible personhood. The broadest ramifications of social creativity are implicit in its structural foundations.

Admittedly, definitions of this order impose a major burden of expectation on any group. They describe ideals against which the routine processes of group life must be constantly projected. The problem of maintaining in practice what is professed in principle is real. It is with grave difficulty that groups which accept its premise avoid compromising its distinctive principle.

For one thing, the popular winds that blow are often not in the direction of free churchism. Being surrounded by a diverse variety of churchly institutions, each of which subscribes generally to the pattern of traditional churches, there is the constant temptation to become also a traditional institution. There are many more incentives toward conformity than there are efforts to maintain a sufficient level of maturity for harmonious cooperation. Free churches are easily persuaded to become just another church.

Again, it may be that the characteristic strength of free churchism often becomes for it a besetting weakness. Living within the awareness that one is actually a constituent factor in the constitution of the church itself, one tends to magnify unduly the importance of the church in his catalogue of priorities. For him the church often becomes an end in itself, all other values becoming subsumed under its province. A true free church thinks of itself as being important but not primary. It is not an end in itself but an accompanying element in faith-experience. It is a by-product of Christian faith-response. In it the posture of selfishness is just as despicable as it is in an individual. If a church is true to its genius it will assume the role of adjective, never a noun renowned. It should occupy an important place in a person's thinking but it will not occupy first place. Viewed in the contest of history this has been a prime fallacy of the churchly enterprise. Free churches appear to be no exception to the rule.

V

The Church and Its Leaders:
First Among Equals

At two points in the life and thought of a free church its basic principles become conspicuously articulate, namely, in the role it ascribes to its leadership and in the significance it attaches to its rites and ceremonies. The manner in which a congregation addresses itself to these two items reveals the levels of its own mature, consistent self-awareness. It follows, therefore, that because these are the points at which it strikes the sharpest contrasts with traditional institutions, it is here that a free church group encounters its gravest levels of misunderstanding and suffers its severest temptation to compromise its unique orientation.

The nature of a church's leadership is inherent in the nature of the church and the character of the church is inherent in the genius of Christian faith. What the church is and what its nature obligates it to do give meaning and value to the service to be engaged upon by its members.

A church which is defined as "a community of disciples" has, by its definition, set limits within which any of its members are qualified to participate in any aspect of the life of the congregation. Discipleship, by which any member is qualified, is what that member holds in common with all other members of the group. This common ground does not imply that all are of equal capacity or ability. It does mean that no one of the group is qualified to exercise authority, *per se*, over others of the congregation.

Leadership in free churches is thus constituted as being *functional*, not *official*. An office to be filled is determined by a type of service to be rendered in and for the group. Persons who are judged by the congregation to be *qualified in ability and disposition* are chosen for the task to be done.

In a true free church circumstance there is no hierarchy of qualification from which that leadership can be drawn. Therefore, leadership must emerge in the person of those who, by consensus, are counted as "first among equals" to be a leader in this kind of congregation. Whatever qualifications that person may achieve for exercising such a prominent role in the group, he is deemed to have achieved those qualifications which, by the same effort, were available as possibilities for any other member of the church.

In a work entitled, *What Is The Church*, (Duke K. McCall, Ed., Nashville: 1958, Ch. III.) we have examined in detail the rise and development of the leadership roles of the first century congregations as reflected in the literature of the New Testament on the basis of the idea that, from the outset, discipleship was conditioned by the sharing of the "good news" of the person and work of Jesus, the Christ. Therefore, those who were familiar with that gospel occupied from the beginning a responsible role as they stood immediately related to the source-springs of the good news they shared. These first disciples were unique and irreplacable in that they had become the persons among whom the Christ had lived and taught. All others, whose discipleship was created by the testimony of these eyewitnesses of the Christ's life and work, became disciples in response to the "good news" but they never became actual participants in the daily life experience created by the Christ as had been the situation in which the apostles had become disciples.

The earliest Christian discipleship was created among the Jewish community of the first century. Jesus was a practicing member of the Jewish synagogue and his associations were chiefly among those who were also devotees of the Jewish religious community. The habitual patterns of their common synagogue experience naturally furnished the designs of the early church aggregations. As a matter of fact, the earliest disciples continued to be associated with their synagogue groups until distinctive differences in their faith outlook became sufficiently prominent to render them unacceptable to their Jewish associates and they were excluded from the synagogue fellowship.

The Jewish patriarchal system, from an early time, created in the synagogue worshipping community a leadership which consisted of the elders of the group. The various items in their traditional routines of worship were divided among the several older men of the group. The patriarchs of the Christian congregations became those who were older, not in chronological age, but more mature in discipleship, more familiar with the gospel and its implications. On the basis of their discipleship they ecame the "disciplers" of others and a leadership function was thereby achieved. Their ability and their willingness to engage in this activity were construed as "gifts" divinely inspired for the benefit of the fledgling community.

Because leadership in a free church community is determined always by the type of service to be rendered, and because all members of the group are qualified by their common experience in faith orientation, it follows that the difference between "officers" and other members of the congregation is a difference of degree and not of kind. A more mature insight into the meaning of the gospel and its implications enables a person to engage in the service that the church determines should be done. Because the cultivation of its spiritual experience in worship is the primary responsibility of the group, the leadership in its corporate worship experience becomes the most conspicuous item in the service roles of its leadership. It falls to the lot of those who, in mature faith orientation, are deemed to be qualified to render this kind of service, and this service defines the role and designates the person or persons who stand at the altar of its worship. These "pastors" occupy a very conspicuous, creative role in the life of the group but the faith dimensions of their own discipleship are not qualitatively other than that which characterizes any other member of the group. In other words, the calibre of their Christian experience is judged to be of sufficient strength to entitle them, in the opinion of the congregation, to exercise leadership among the group's members but that level of experience is also available and is to be encouraged in every other member of the church.

From an early period in church history forces both within and on the outside of the new enterprise encouraged vast changes in the concept of the church, changes which carried the church enterprise far from its free church character. These changes also created corresponding alterations in the status of church leadership. The focus was shifted from personal faith response to institutional authority in matters of religious experience. Those who stood within the newly developed authoritarian structure were endowed with "the power of the keys," the authority to forgive or to condemn. Service in the church was exercised by a "clergy" successionally endowed with the divine gift of administering all aspects of personal religious experience. Levels of privilege and participation in the life and work of the religion were the consequence. Those in roles of leadership no longer stood on the common level of discipleship as their sole qualification but in a special category over and above the average participant in church affairs.

It goes without saying that the person who stands to lead in the cultivation of the finest aspects of spiritual experience creates for himself a favored position in the acceptance and respect of those whom he serves. It is a grave temptation, therefore, for the leader of a church to think of himself "more highly than he ought think," to assume a commanding status in the life of his fellows. Those who lead congregations of a free church persuasion, over a considerable period of time, gradually tend in the

direction of a traditional ministry. Their service
neatly parallels that of those whose work is "official"
in other congregations. The temptation is intensified
by the fact that the ceremony by which free churches
designate their leaders is virtually the same as those
employed in ecclesiastical institutions, namely the
ceremony of ordination.

Traditional ecclesiastical groups ordain their leaders by what is called "investiture," that is, there is
transmitted to leaders the authority of the church to
engage in its leadership. Free church thinking accepts
none of this. On the basis of discipleship a person is
marked by a simple ceremony as being acknowledged
as having the *ability* and *disposition* to lead and, by
the consent of the membership, is designated as
leader. By this device he becomes "first among
equals," being asked to move to a place of prominence
among those who, literally, are his equals.

In most church circles, from the most rigid types of
ecclesiastical administration to the freest church
bodies, the ceremony of ordination is practically the
same, namely, prayer and the "laying on of hands."
There seems to be first century precedent for this.
However, the ceremony was not, in the first century,
limited to ordination for leadership. It was practiced
also for discipleship generally as the symbolic occasion of "Holy Spirit enduement." This would seem to
dilute considerably the specifics of the biblical tradition as far as an exclusive rite for the designation of
church leadership.

In any event, the two parts of the simple ceremony,
as engaged in by free churches, are virtually two
ways of expressing the same thing. They engage in a
symbolism of prayerful enduement, by laying on

hands, and a vocal prayer also. In other words, the two aspects of the ceremony amount to a *prayer said* and a *prayer done.*

Historically, free churches have sometimes avoided the semblance of creating an "official" clergy by declining the formalities of ordination altogether. Charles Haddon Spurgeon, a prominent British free churchman, refused to accept ordination at the hands of his fellow churchmen. His jocose remark was: "I do not want empty hands laid on my empty head." By this remark he identified himself clearly with a disdain for any kind of hierarchical rank in a free church circumstance.

Dietrich Bonhoeffer, the twentieth century member of the German opposition to Hitler's Third Reich, who was executed by the German government just prior to the Allied liberation of Germany, was committed, through numerous publications during the period of World War II, to the idea of the spontaneity and vitality of personal religion. His disdain for the institutional structures into which Christianity had been crystallized was such that he advocated seriously the propagation of the contagion of faith apart from the role of a professional clergy. He feared that it would not be possible for the dynamics of the religion to assert themselves creatively in the world so long as its leading edge was embodied in those who were leaders in faith-experience by the formalities of professionalism. It is obviously an extreme position with reference to church leadership but it does serve to mark distinctly the trend toward an objective approach to faith activity. It is worthy criticism of the development which has transpired in the Christian world as a whole, a development which free churchism has not avoided with any degree of success.

Developments in twentieth century civilization, particularly in the West, have created in every ramification of societal relationships an emphasis on quantitative efficiency, this to an extent that the contemporary church has been modified decidedly in this direction. In many quarters this trend has been described by such terms as "the secularization of the church." It is too much to expect that a free church congregation, however deeply it may be committed to free church principles, would escape the inroads of this development. There are few free church groups who would risk the posture of being a magnetic faith-oriented church, endeavoring to engage upon its task solely in terms of the techniques inherent in its faith dynamics, apart from the crusades and campaigns which are largely devised by the techniques of modern commercial salesmanship. To raise the question is to be required to raise again the reason for the church's being, however. In a subsequent discussion of the church in the world a great deal more will be said about this problem. Here it is sufficient to affirm that, in any area of endeavor, the method of operation deserves to be devised in terms of the basic purposes which are implicit in the undertaking. It may be that free churchism as it is currently pursued has largely reversed this set of priorities.

Developments in a scholarly understanding of the Bible and an adequate interpretation of it have made it necessary for anyone who would become qualified to exercise an able leadership in a contemporary church to invest a great deal of interest and energy in preparation. Just as the level of cultural orientation of the average member of modern society has been increased tremendously, there has come to be an increasingly high premium on the level of insight on the part of those who would stand in a leadership position in any societal institution. This includes the church. Its ministers are obligated to become acquainted with the life situation of people generally, to become capable of addressing themselves to the needs and aspirations of people generally, furnishing that element of inspiration and devotion that faith insures.

Again, this does not remove a leader of the church from the rank of church folk. What he comes to understand about biblical matters is available to every other person in the church. In fact, however facile he may become in "rightly dividing the word" to that extent he is obligated to share his insights with the humblest member of the congregation. By becoming an "educated minister" he is under additional obligation to share his insights with all the rest. His adequate leadership shall consist primarily in his disposition and ability to bring to all the rest the depths of his own attainments.

The free churches have followed generally the pattern of leadership roles as reflected in biblical language. They have chosen pastors, evangelists, and deacons, plus a wide variety of what some call "officers of necessity" such as treasurers and organizational leaders. The responsibilities of each officer of any group have been conditioned upon the measure of service expected of each officer. In the order of rank the pastor has traditionally stood first. This is being qualified considerably in recent decades in the program of larger congregations in maintaining a plurality of "ministers." In any event, a free church premise will delineate a church's official life in terms of the democratic processes of discipleship.

In many circles much controversary is occasioned by the distinctions drawn from "ordained" ministries versus "unordained" ministries. This reflects the extent to which ordination is taken to be a device for the creation of a level of authority or status in the churches. If the free church principle is scrupulously observed, ordination is an *acknowledgement,* not an endowment or bestowal. Therefore, if the several services of the congregation are called for, then any process by which those who render these services are recognized will limit the extent to which ordination has significance in the free churches. In other words, if there is a service to be rendered and someone is qualified and willing to render that service, and the congregation gives consent or approval, then that person has become an "officer" of the church. Variations in the status or prominence given to the several servants is inherent in the evaluation of the services rendered, not in the different levels of the persons engaged upon them.

A complicating element in all of this matter of an "ordained" ministry is the fact that officers of the churches are given certain "official" status in public affairs, such as acting as agents of the state. In conducting marriage ceremonies, for example, a person's qualifications in church circles enables that person to engage in the marriage ceremony as an authorized agent of the government. These government proscriptions are based on the traditional patterns of church leadership. They reflect ordination by investiture, not the democratic principle of free church economy. For convenience free church officers have acquiesced in the routine regulations governing such matters. They have come to think of themselves in terms of the traditional pattern of leadership, however. Few have ventured to interpret their own role in church apart from their role as government agent.

Much controversy has also been occasioned by the increasingly frequent ordination of women as well as men to leadership roles in free churches. Again, this changing situation is but a reflection of the changing societal circumstance. The churches increasingly ask women to engage in its service. That free churches should formally recognize that service is logical and legitimate. It is another instance where traditional practices have been imposed upon the function of basic principles.

VI

The Church and Its Symbols

As indicated above the manner in which a church construes its rites and ceremonies becomes one of the most revealing aspects of its real character and purpose. By the time the free church movement arose the tides of a long history had carried both the character of the church and its ceremonial practices far from what free churchmen thought both should be. Their sixteenth century "congregations of disciples" stood in stark contradiction to the all but universal tradition of an ecclesiastical institution which claimed prerogatives for dispensing the benefit of divine grace.

For centuries the traditional church had maintained an elaborate sacerdotal-sacramental system through which it bestowed its blessings. By means of seven specific rites, called sacraments, it purported to fashion in the individual a satisfactory faith orientation. At the creative center of its sacraments stood baptism and the eucharist, together calculated to constitute the cutting edge of all satisfactory spiritual wellbeing.

In reassessing the entire concept of discipleship the free churchmen also found it necessary to alter

the entire concept of the two rites. They evidenced
no inclination to neglect baptism and the Lord's
Supper, the term they used to refer to the eucharist,
for they found both prominent in the literature of
the first century church. They reinterpreted both so
as to make them fit within the framework of their
notion of an individual, voluntary faith-response to
the Christian gospel.

Baptism was acknowledged as a legitimate initiatory ceremony to be engaged upon as the individual
was inducted into the congregation. It stood closely
related to the experience of becoming a disciple. It
was easily construed, therefore, as being administered in a churchly circumstance.

It was from their insistence on baptism being
administered as a definite part of congregational
association rather than as a vehicle through which
salvation benefits were to be acquired that the earliest free churchmen derived the name, Anabaptists.
In the eyes of the gainsaying traditional churchmen
they were "rebaptizers"; they were churches which
required a second baptism. By rejecting baptism as it
had been customarily administered the free churches
did require that it be administered according to their
concept of its relation to salvation. Regardless of
previous baptismal experience, therefore, the Anabaptists insisted on persons receiving baptism *after*
their experience of salvation. To them this was not a
second baptism but baptism which was properly
construed, a rite with an altogether different
meaning and purpose.

For centuries past the method of baptism as practiced by the traditional church had been that of

affusion. Affusion had become so deeply ingrained in the perspective of the post-medieval Christianity it was adopted without apparent question by the Anabaptists. For more than a century they continued the practice before any suggestion was made regarding a different mode. It was not disturbed by all the radical departures which the free churchmen made in the traditional churchly endeavor until a change was proposed by the English in the seventeenth century. An apparent drift in the direction of literalism became the occasion of the introduction of immersion. Increasingly, particularly in both the Baptist and the Disciples heirs of the British development, immersion has become the mode employed by those who insist on "believers' baptism."

Among the several groups which have come to insist on believers' baptism by immersion there have developed widespread differences in the interpretation of the rite. Perhaps the majority opinion is that the rite is a symbolic observance, immersion in water symbolizing the death-resurrection of Jesus, plus the additional picture of the death of the disciple to his former sinful condition and his recreation to a new life in faith. Upon the basis of this interpretation many free churches will agree to administer immersion only for baptism. Heretofore their restrictive thought on the subject has prompted them to require immersion of those who come to them from congregations in which they did not receive immersion. More recently many congregations have come to accept transfers of membership from such churches without requiring immersion. Most of these churches have continued to administer only immersion, however.

In American free church circles a considerable body of congregations, principally those who are followers of Alexander Campbell and Barton W. Stone, have emphasized immersion as "an act of Obedience." One must "obey the gospel," they insist, in order to be saved. All of the churches of this persuasion have continued to maintain immersion as the mode of baptism.

The most strictly legalistic interpretation of immersion baptism among free church people was proposed by the leadership of what has come to be known in American Baptist circles as the Landmark movement. It was inaugurated by James R. Graves and others during the mid-nineteenth century. Distinctly high church in character, the Landmark leadership proposed to legitimize all church affairs, including an emphasis on what they construed as "scriptural baptism," by appealing to what they defined as an unbroken "apostolic authority." They sought to prove an unbroken succession of Baptist church life from the first century. They prepared a history of true church lineage, regressively beginning with a congregation in Arkansas and identifying successive generations of churches, by name and specific geographic location, to the origin of the true churches in first century discipleship. Valid immersion baptism was measured altogether in terms of whether it was done "by a proper administrator, in a proper church, by a proper method, to a properly qualified candidate." It is fair to say that though this kind of validity has long since been abandoned by most Baptist congregations, the influence of this kind of in-group exclusiveness has continued to characterize large areas of Baptist life.

For those who seek to interpret immersion so as to avoid authoritarianism it is construed altogether in terms of the meaning that can be ascribed to it in the immediate circumstance of its administration. In a sense parallel to the individual responsibility for faith experience, the meaning of baptism is identified largely as the meaning that is given to it by the person who is baptized. He brings to it a fresh perspective which has been created by his new sense of loyalty to Christ and he manifests that commitment by this outward sign. It becomes for him an occasion for witnessing his inner experience and it gives testimony to others of his inner spiritual affinities. His baptism is given meaning by the sincerity of his commitment.

Tertullian, the third century Roman legalist, employed the analogy of the military ceremony, the "sacramentum," to illustrate the significance of baptism. The Roman legions, which were composed chiefly of mercernary soldiers, were required to take an oath of allegiance to the Roman authority by being processed in a formal ceremony. The ritual consisted essentially in the requirement to walk under a standard, placed deliberately so as to make it necessary for the soldier to bow his head as he walked through, reciting an oath as he did. Tertullian described baptism as a Christian "sacramentum," an oath-taking experience, a ceremony in which the new disciple put on the uniform of the Christian army.

Notwithstanding the non-redemptive protestations of the immersionists, those who practice this mode often insist on it with such emphasis as to leave the impression that they, too, ascribe approximately the same significance to it. They inveigh vigorously against other forms of the ordinance, contending that in history these others were too closely associated with baptismal regeneration. It is an awkward and delicate process that emphasizes immersion, making it requisite to membership in the church while placing as much emphasis as the free churches do on personal salvation outside the circle of church membership.

J. L. Dagg, writing at the time in the nineteenth century when the Graves-Landmark movement was in its ascendency, was sensitive to this problem:

> It is our duty, while rendering punctillious obedience to all the commandments of God to regard the forms and ceremonies of religion as of far less importance than its moral truths and precepts.
>
> One of the earliest corruptions of Christianity consisted of magnifying the importance of its ceremonies, and of ascribing to them a saving efficacy. With this superstitious reverence of outward forms, a tendency was introduced to corrupt these forms. . . . We are often charged with attaching too much importance to immersion; but the notion that baptism possesses a sacramental efficacy finds no advocates in our ranks. . . . To give due prominence to spirituality above all outward ceremony, is an important service to which God has called our denomination.

(*Manual of Theology*, Second Part. Charleston, S.C.: Southern Baptist Publication Society, 1858, p. 301.)

It may be that over a considerable period of time it is not possible to maintain as much emphasis on immersion as many of the free churches give to it without creating the impression in the mind of those who practice it as well as the impression made on others that baptism is essential for the inauguration of a satisfactory faith experience. It is well to note the circumstance in which such a position is being maintained. In all of twentieth century Christianity only approximately nine percent practice immersion. This minority includes all branches of the Eastern Church which, from an early period, adopted infant baptist by "trine immersion." When the aggregate of Orthodox membership is excluded there remains but a very small minority of those who can claim to be lineal heirs of the early "re-baptizers." Matters such as these are not to be determined by mathematical proportions, of course, but the few who insist on immersion are so negligible in number their emphasis on it is calculated to wrench it out of all reasonable context. It is for this reason that I have reminded successive generations of students that it is an exceedingly delicate operation to tell new converts that they *must* be immersed, but that it is not calculated to be an imperative in their spiritual pilgrimage.

It may be that the Society of Friends, the Quakers, have arrived at the most logical judgment regarding the practice of the ordinances. They have given up on trying to rescue them from the dismemberment they have suffered in the past. They do not observe either ordinance. They are to be commended for the fact that they do not spend their spiritual energies on mere pietistic devotion. They are among the most enthusiastic of all Christian bodies in applying their inner faith to the practical affairs of worldly lore. They discern so clearly that faith is a matter of internal, spiritual experience, however, they forego the obligation to engage in the external rites which are common to most communions.

It was not a Quaker, but an eminent party of the Congregational movement in Great Britain, who early in this century came to approximately the same conclusion regarding the ceremonies. A. M. Fairbairn, inured by constant contest with the State Church and its practices, remarked that the ceremonials of churches are really kindergarten routines of religion. He thought they might be appropriate for those who dwell at that level of spiritual maturity but that they become relatively less useful to those who become responsibly integrated in faith experience.

As has been indicated, the major alteration of the seven-sacrament system of the traditional church was their deliberate effort to divest them of any semblance of saving efficacy. They became, literally, ordinances, not sacraments. As in the case of baptism the Lord's Supper became a ceremony largely symbolic in meaning.

They employed bread and wine as the emblem but there was no suggestion as to any problem whether the rite should be observed "in both kinds." Among the several groups there have occurred considerable variations relative to the manner of its observance. In some circles much emphasis is given to the qualifications of the participants. In extreme instances the privilege has been limited to the members of the local congregation, invoking the principle that only those should participate who are under the "disciplinary direction" of the congregation. It followed that in many instances some members of the local church were denied the privilege, being judged as less than worthy in their "Christian walk."

As this practice of close regulation of the observance has come under the influence of the high church separateness of denominational alignment the qualification for participation has been defined as membership "in churches of like faith and order." This is obviously an extension of the close communion concept, the concept of church being somewhat subsumed under the idea of a particular denomination.

Among free churches generally, however, the ordinance has come to assume the proportions of "communion," with the emphasis on a symbolism available to "all who know themselves to be disciples." Their sense of unity is enhanced by an emphasis on the concept of Christ as the central idea of the symbolism rather than a unity contingent upon the particular affiliation of the participants. People of this persuasion take Paul's admonition regarding "unworthy" observance in the Corinthian congregation to mean, primarily, that when with ulterior purposes they observed the Supper they vitiated the concept of the Christ who was being celebrated.

Some free church groups arrange for the celebration of the ordinance at every "sabbath occasion" of the congregation. This practice is especially prevalent among those who are of the Disciples tradition. The Disciples of Christ, the Churches of Christ, and the several related bodies observe the ordinance at every Sunday morning service of worship.

Notwithstanding the variations in the manner of observing the Lord's Supper, however, free churches have maintained consistently a non-sacramental significance for the rite. They have continued to set it in a framework closely related to the anti-ecclesiastical structures of church life as they think these deserve to be.

VII

A Free Church among Other Churches

To this point in the discussion we have been occupied chiefly with examining the free church principle as it functions in a particular congregation. It is appropriate to an understanding of the entire perspective of the movement to view the relations of a free church to other churches. This entails what has come to be known as its denominational connections as well as its relations with churches which are not of its own persuasion, its ecumenical relationships.

From the time of their establishment in this country the general tenor of the various free church bodies was largely determined by the mindset which they had acquired in their Old World moorings. Baptists in New England, for example, were remarkably similar to the Baptists of Great Britain. The Congregationalists here maintained about the same complexion as that of the "Brownites" of England from which they had sprung.

As had been true in Great Britain, the strongest ties which they began to develop here were with "churches of their own kind." Whatever variations on the free church theme had been created heretofore they transported to the New World. Each peculiarity which formerly had been acquired now served to distinguish each of them from the rest and furnished the basis for the group's associations with others of their own persuasion. They found considerable psychological comfort in the presence of major agreement in belief and practice.

Ahlstrom is of the opinion that these lines which now distinguished them they inherited almost altogether from the Old World. In an elaborate analysis of American Christianity he contends that the several New World denominations, with few exceptions, brought with them the specifics of particular church identity, that they merely transferred to American soil their earlier characteristics. (Ahlstrom, Sydney, *A Religious History of the American People.* New Haven: Yale University Press, 1972.)

Notwithstanding these distinctions which characterized the American congregations, however, there soon developed among them one feature common to all, namely, an inclination toward particularism. This spirit of individualism became prominent in all American institutions. It was inspired, no doubt, by the atmosphere of independence in which all were developed. It was a disposition so conspicuous as even to have been engendered in groups whose tradition had been that of a rigid pattern of ecclesiastical connectionalism. Historians of the Anglican-Episcopal Church, for example, allege that American Episcopalians are individualistic in ways not found in their Anglican ancestry.

The frontier circumstance under which all early American churches originated resulted in all interchurch association among them being meager and occasional. The churches of any particular persuasion were widely scattered and contacts between them were difficult. Any association they knew was necessarily contrived.

The earliest groupings grew directly out of this pioneer circumstance. A sense of isolation and loneliness prompted particular congregations to seek the fellowship of other groups. Invitations were extended to neighboring bodies to meet with them for mutual aid and encouragement. Entire congregations sometimes accepted such invitations, coming to camp nearby for several days for programs of worship and discussion. There was a dearth of ministers among them, the leadership of particular groups being furnished principally by itinerant ministers. Preaching, therefore, became a prominent part of all such programs.

An example of this kind of meeting was the assembling of the five Baptist churches in the Philadelphia area, once a year for several years, the several groups camping together. Eventually an informal organization was devised, coming to be known as The Philadelphia Association. It was the earliest inter-church organization among Baptists in America. Its informal character is reflected in the fact that for several years after its formation it participated in these joint sessions without electing a moderator. All those present were Baptists. Nevertheless, their sessions were interspersed with lengthy periods devoted to a discussion of their differences.

This earliest Baptist organization was developed from the annual "association" of the congregations, thus giving the title of Association to a new "denominational" body. It has been maintained from that time to the present as the level of denominational life of most free church groups in this country has followed essentially this regional type of development.

Each free church aggregation in this country has progressed from its meager beginnings in Colonial history to become an elaborate, closely knit organization. The story of the growth of each group has paralleled neatly the developments which have taken place in the culture as a whole. As the nation became increasingly populous each church group has grown and has become increasingly complex in its organizational structure.

The American culture has moved along lines of rather well-defined stratification, its various subdivisions having been fashioned according to the variations which have occurred in its economic development. It eventually became commonplace to designate its cultural groups as being "upper class," "middle class," or "lower class," the designations being made on the basis of relative economic success. These social categories have, in turn, tended to generate in the populace corresponding levels of social maturity, affording relative facility or discouragement to the members of each category.

As strange as it should seem the growth of denominational organizations in American church life has followed precisely these lines of economic growth in the culture as a whole. Niebuhr in his work, *The Social Sources of Denominationalism*, (New York: Henry Holt and Company, 1929), describes incisively the manner in which this growth has occurred. He takes careful account of the fragmentation of both culture and church into such subdivisions as "the

immigrant church," the churches of the "disinheri-
ted," "the color divisions of the church," etc. Whatever else these configurations may suggest, it is
difficult to avoid the judgment that in the course of
its life in the New World the church has come to be
influenced largely by factors which are external to its
true nature. Circumstances over and beyond its own
character have come to determine its life in the
American community.

Niebuhr insists, however

> that the evils of denominationalism do not lie in this differ-
> entiation of churches and sects . . . On the contrary, the
> rise of new sects to champion the uncompromising ethics
> of Jesus and to "preach the gospel to the poor" has again
> and again been the effective means of recalling the church
> to its mission.
>
> The evil of denominationalism lies in the conditions
> which make the rise of sects . . . . necessary, in the failure of
> the churches to transcend the social conditions which
> fashion them into caste organizations . . . to resist the
> temptation of making their own self-preservation and
> extension the primary object to their endeavor.
>
> The denominations, churches, sects, are sociological
> groups whose principle of differentiation is to be sought in
> their conformity to the order of social classes and castes.
>
> Denominations thus represent the moral failure of Chris-
> tianity. . . . They are emblems of the victory of the world
> over the church.

[Op. cit., pp. 21ff.]

It is the development of church life on this order
which has prompted some to call denominationalism
in American Christianity "the Babylonian Captivity
of the church." Because the church has allowed its
contours to become fashioned so largely by social
forces, forces which are not only outside the church
but which, in many instances, are actually inimical to

its character and purpose. For example, it is a somber thought that several major denominations in the United States, groups which have operated for more than a century, actually trace their origin to the social crisis over slavery. Their forebears separated themselves from parent bodies by insisting on a pro-slavery position in the conflict.

In contrast to this overall condition of twentieth century denominationalism the recitations of Hans Küng on the real nature and purpose of the church stand in bold relief:

> The church then is the whole community of those who believe in Christ, in which all see themselves as people of God, body of Christ, building of the Spirit. What really counts in this community is not any privilege, or birth, class, race, or office. The kind of "office" a person holds or even whether he holds office at all it is not important. What matters is whether, and to what extent a person is simply and solely a "believer": Whether and How far he believes, serves, hopes and commits himself in the spirit of Jesus Christ in a wholly concrete way.
>
> . . . A Christian needs no priest in addition to Christ as mediator in the innermost center of the temple, with God himself. For in the last resort he has been given an immediate access to God which no ecclesiastical authority can disturb, still less take away from him. No one has any power to judge, control or order decisions which fall within the innermost sphere. . . . "Church," great or small, is the whole community of faith which proclaims the Gospel — often more through humble people than through hierarchs and theologians, more by deed than by words — in order to awaken faith in Jesus Christ, provoke commitment to his Spirit, make the church present in the world in everyday Christian witness and so carry on the cause of Jesus Christ.

(Hans Küng, *On Being a Christian*, pp. 481f.)

A major cause of the development of denomina-tionalism among the churches was the assumption of large responsibilities on the part of the churches, more than could be sustained by any particular congregation. This occurred early in American history as church groups undertook to establish schools.

The Colonial government was established on the basis of the qualification of the ordinary citizen to engage in a system of self-government. At the time this kind of expectation was being imposed no special provision was made to cultivate in the average citizen these elemental qualifications. The education of citi-zens had posed no real problem for the class of elitists who were the framers of the system. They took the initiative in providing education for the members of their household by private instruction. Many of this group imported tutors from France and England for this service. This was beyond the means of the average household; consequently no educational facilities were available for them.

The churches, particularly members of the free churches, whose primary approach to the human situation was an appeal to the responsible participa-tion of the individual, became cognizant of this void and began movements to supply the need. Most of the institutions of higher education which were inaugurated during the Colonial period were begun under church auspices. This fact called for an imme-diate consolidation of church resources. Educational associations for the purpose of supporting the schools, composed of church folk, sprang up in many areas of the country.

Public interest in education became aroused and, as an afterthought, government leadership initiated a system of schools under state auspices available to the general public. The growth of this system of free public education in the United States has been phenomenal.

Church schools, as such, in large numbers have continued to exist but the mortality rate among all of those which have been founded has been extremely high. The expansion of public education has also forced them into a different role in society. They no longer enjoy the position of filling a vacuum in educational facilities and are required, in theory, to justify their existence largely as agencies of church extension. With the development of thorough processes of accreditation and standardization which have become universal, all schools, public and private, are required to offer practically the same program of education and are operated in direct competition with each other. Only the strongest of the church related institutions survive and these are maintained largely by the momentum of their tradition and as objects of private philanthropy. On an average, churches of all persuasions now contribute less than five percent to the support of the schools which bear their name.

By the beginning of the twentieth century the "success pattern" of American life had been well established. It was intensely interrelated and was largely *quantitative* in its standard of measurement. The strength of most institutions had come to be counted largely in terms of its size and the resources it controlled. The denominational dimensions of the typical church group had been carried along on this wave of secularism. It began to accept this same principle and operated largely in terms of it. As a matter of fact, by that time the central dynamics of the average congregation had been shifted from the local church to its denominational organization. The qualitative standards of the marketplace had become the standard of the church as well.

This process of solidifying the congregations into a larger denominational organization progressed to the point that these blocks of free churches became practically indistinguishable from the traditional ecclesiastical institutions. In theory the free churches retained a nominal basis of "local church autonomy" but, by and large, their corporate interests overshadowed their particular endeavors. It has progressed to the point that only in theory does one distinguish between "the Episcopal Church" and "the Baptist Church" in the parlance of the marketplace.

Early in the twentieth century someone aptly defined the Southern Baptist Convention as "a religious bank chartered under the laws of the State of Georgia, in 1845, for the purpose of collecting and distributing funds for missions, education and benevolence." This definition reflects respect for the free church principle to which Baptists subscribe. It is fair to add that it has been a long time since the definition has been repeated. In actual practice all of the members of all of the churches of this communion, in so far as it is possible, are enlisted in all of the "programs" of the denomination, *programs which are invariably initiated at the denominational level* which are administered by an organizational structure that is as general and all-inclusive as if it had been promoted by the most solidly connected eccle-

siastical institution. It is a commonplace to judge
each unit of the structure by the numbers represented in its membership and its financial resources.
So largely have the internal and external aspects of a
church's character become equated that the technique of improving its internal life is virtually equated
with the enlarging of its external features. It is with
exceeding difficulty that the reverse of this process is
achieved.

Students of first century Christianity are impressed
with what strong cords of love and mutual trust the
earliest disciples were bound to each other. Their
mutual understanding and their preferences for each
other were sufficient to sustain them in seasons of
persecution and peril. These bonds served also to
distinguish them from all others, from all those who
were outside the circle of their fellowship. Many have
observed this pristine condition and have lamented,
therefore, that the time soon came when some disciples found it necessary to take serious account of the
differences between themselves and others who likewise professed the Christian faith, but whose beliefs
and practices they considered to be inimical to their
cause. From an early period their bonds began to be
loosened and cleavages appeared in their fellowship.
This kind of development has not been ameliorated
with the passing of centuries. Unfortunately, many
such divisions have been occasioned by disagreements over matters which were not weighty but
trivial.

Admittedly, any system of faith-orientation which
places great premium on responsible individualism
in matters religious has within it the seed of independence and poses the possibility of dissent. The free

church movement is peculiarly vulnerable at this point. It had its rise in a vigorous protest against a coercive authoritarianism which, by a system of external pressures, bound people together in church life. Free churchmen who were freed to choose their own way acknowledge that in any cooperative endeavor it is solely the strength of their agreements which bind them together. Where they disagree, therefore, these disagreements become consequential, whether they be weighty or trivial.

Free churchism is not an unbridled individualism. It is based, instead, on a level of mature self-discipline which is calculated to furnish a trustworthy fellowship. It would seem that any group which lives by the mature qualifications of the invididual would be inclined to look with respect upon the embodiment of this principle wherever it is found. Unfortunately this posture of mutual maturity has not achieved a universally operable system of ecumenical relationships among the several free church bodies. Some of them are positive and open toward others while others are exclusive and separate in outlook.

The Congregationalists, the Disciples of Christ, and some Baptists, for example, have developed close ecumenical relationships. On the other hand, other Baptists bodies, notably Southern Baptists, have become exclusive and separate. It is advisable, therefore, to examine the disposition of members of each of these groups as we look to the fellowship of free churches with each other.

The circumstances under which Congregationalism was introduced into Colonial America forged in this group an ambivalent pattern. Their background in England was that of a typical free church society. It came into New England, however, under the aegis of a strained, highly provincial Colonial government which determined that it would also become highly provincial. At an early time it became the established church in Massachusetts and, with Anglicanism, enjoys the dubious reputation of having been the only establishments in the New World. It was the state church of Massachusetts until 1834. Eventually it recovered its English background disposition and has become thoroughly positive and inclusive in outlook. It has become among the most congenial of American denominations toward ecumenism.

The Disciples of Christ churches were from the beginning deeply involved in the schismatic conflicts of the early nineteenth century which created in it a rather checkered pattern of development. Ironically, Alexander Campbell and Barton W. Stone, the instigators of the movement, came forth to champion the cause of peace among the churches. Having become exasperated by the provincialism in American Christianity, they set about to unify the communions "by the restoration of first century religion." The literalistic biblicism of these leaders proved to be divisive, resulting in heated controversy rather than peace.

Fortunately, when a major division occurred in the movement at the middle of the century, what at that time became the major group of the Disciples was persuaded by the peace-making intentions of the founders. This group was committed to an open, respectful disposition toward all other churches and has continued to take a consistently constructive part in efforts for church union. They are unequivocal in their spirit of cooperation and encouragement.

They are a good example of the spirit of free church-ism. Manifesting a strong confidence in the biblical moorings of their faith, with a sense of security they maintain an inclusive attitude toward all other churches.

Unfortunately this has not been true of the right wing of the followers of Campbell and Stone. These have continued to embrace the most conservative and quarrelsome inclinations of the founders and must be listed among those who are the least inclined to favor ecumenical ties with other groups.

The British background of the Baptists was similar to that of the Congregationalists. They came to America at about the same time and with the same general outlook. Perhaps it could be said that they were characterized at the outset with among the strongest dispositions toward toleration of all the free church groups. From the outset they were buffeted by hostile elements in the colonies, particularly in instances where there was an established church. They were both persecuted and prosecuted and by the exigencies of this circumstance they were required to examine regularly the foundations upon which they functioned. The saga of Roger Williams and the founding of the Rhode Island Colony are conspicuous items in the annals of American Baptist history. With strength thus engendered they were admirably equipped for the task of working on the American frontier where they served with considerable success.

When the issue of slavery became acute American Baptists were divided. The Southern group, which withdrew from the main body in 1845 to organize a separate denomination, did so because they insisted on maintaining a pro-slavery position in all of their church connections. As indicated above, the Land-mark-fundamentalist wave of the nineteenth century served to solidify their ranks and to alter appreciably their attitude toward themselves and toward all others.

Within the rapidly expanding conditions of the region this Southern group has been parlayed into becoming the largest Protestant denomination in the United States. Undergirded by impressive resources and with strong institutional organization, Southern Baptists press their point of view upon increasing areas of the world's populace. They hold themselves carefully aloof from any serious alliance with other church bodies. They contend that all such entangling alliances are a compromise of their church and its message.

This attitude, at times, proves to be a rather awkward posture to maintain, especially at a time when in so many quarters of the Christian world one finds an increasing subscription to the basic princi-ples which Baptists espouse. A jealous regard for a certain church tends to blur the image of the faith-orientation of personal religion which has been the identifying idea of the free church movement. Baptist forebears rejected the idea of placing "church" in the primary place in religious priorities, denying that it is indispensable to satisfactory religious experience, contending that any situation in which church becomes primary creates an aberration of evangeli-cal faith. It may be that the twentieth century Southern Baptist emphasis on church presses the idea of church considerably beyond that normally sanctioned by a legitimate free church situation.

This brief sketch of representative free church bodies is perhaps sufficient to exemplify the notion that, although the several groups lay claim to a common background, even so, among these closely related bodies are to be found diametrical attitudes toward any common ground of faith and practice.

VIII

The Free Church in the World

The free church came into Western culture as a new idea in religion, proposing to express itself through a different kind of institution. Normally new ideas, if they are worthy, are given a certain plausibility by the passing of time; the implications of their intent and purpose are given opportunity to become explicit. By being subjected to the processes of history whatever claims they may have made become justified in the effects they have created. Eventually they may even become conspicuous by the presence in the culture of the new currents which they have generated.

After functioning within the culture for more than three hundred years it is now reasonable to ask whether the free church, with its new idea, couched in a different kind of institution, has, to any appreciable degree, been able to realize its promise. How effectively have the singular insights with which it began modified the religious framework of the West? Again, notwithstanding the relative prosperity of some segments of the movement, in what measure have the character and prospect for human life been improved by these centuries of its ministry? Having existed

101

sufficiently long to have begun to justify itself, it is therefore appropriate to begin to assess its status and to evaluate whatever contributions it may have made during this period.

In the contemporary circumstance it is difficult to separate so as to identify specific contributions made by any particular group. Evaluation must be made in the context of vast changes which have occurred throughout the culture in recent decades. In the complex conditions it is sometimes difficult to determine which factors have been creative and which have been created by the currents of change which have been flowing. It is a period which is often described as being "modern" in that all aspects of it have been altered measurably. Across the West there has flowed a tide in which "all boats have been lifted," as is often remarked. For example, all aspects of the culture have enjoyed the largess of the scientific revolution, the seminal factor in the creation of the modern socio-economic epoch. Communication and transportation facilities have been accelerated and intensified to such extent that in a brief interval the entire world has been enveloped in one interrelated and interdependent whole. All institutions, especially churches which depend so largely on these agents as means of propagation, have been given unusual encouragement. In all of these changes the dynamics of so-called secularism have been tremendously effectual. It is fair to insist that the role of religion has also been prominent. All religious institutions have participated and, in turn, all have been extensively altered in the process.

It may be that coming into the modern era free churches enjoyed advantages considerably above

those which came to most religious groups. Unlike
most others it was an indirect by-product of the
Renaissance perspective; in a sense it might be said
to have become symptomatic of the spiritual core of
the new order. By nature, therefore, it was peculiarly
qualified to exercise a creative role in the new regime.
In keeping with its modern disposition it rejected the
authoritarian strictures of medievalism, and assisted
in throwing off the yoke of the imperial religious
body which had been dominant for more than a
millennium. Like most modern groups its value
norms rested upon a new foundation, namely, the
responsible participation of the newly awakened,
capable human individual. It defined satisfactory
religious experience in terms of an encounter of that
capable individual with the divine in meaningful,
revelatory experience. In character this new church
was qualified to speak the language of modernity, to
address itself effectively to the deepest aspirations of
a new humanity, the inhabitants of the new age of
the world.

The religious situation in the West may be said to
have been affected in some degree by the fact that, in
theory at least, such a group as the free church now
exists. Here is a religious body, steeped in the spirit of
modernity, purporting to be composed of a consti-
tuency which it acquires in a different manner,
where formerly no such church existed. When viewed
in the context of traditional church history the new
body might be said to epitomize the culture's emanci-
pation. Its innovative dimensions equip it to speak to
the new age with a voice which is not strange. In
whatever extent it is able to give expression to its
real character it is able to address the modern mind

with a version of the gospel which is reasonably suited to the inclinations of the modern mind. Unencumbered, and in simple, straightforward terms, it is prepared to invoke upon the populace of the new age the highest moral and spiritual resources of the Christian faith. When true to itself it is a body "lean and vigorous," capable of bringing a message and a church less cluttered by the trappings which institutional religion has accumulated through its long history.

It is to be lamented that when the free church is examined in terms of what it proposed to be and do its life and work must be reckoned as having left much to be desired. Judged by its own assumptions the movement as a whole has fallen far short of its theoretical character and promise.

For one thing it has failed to maintain much more than a semblance of the fresh, creative innovation with which it was begun. It had not ventured far into the modern era before its distinctives were compromised. The sharp edges of its original intentions soon became seriously eroded. Before it had made much of a mark on the religious complexion of the age it had settled into a comfortable place among the traditional churches, hardly distinguishable from those against whose tenets its forebears had protested. It soon found itself being "just another church" among the several churches which are available as options in the average community.

The chief source of this aberration is not difficult to identify. Like most religious bodies the free church was victimized by the fallacy of confusing the "idea" of the church with its "institution." It failed to maintain the clear distinction which was the central conviction of its founders, namely, the notion that faith-response, which is the *sine qua non* of all evangelical Christianity, is itself the creator of the church. To become confused at this point is to tend, always, to equate the techniques of discipleship, the *internals* of a religion, with its *externals*, whatever societal form a group may choose to employ. It is a confusion which invariably results in magnifying the church beyond reasonable proportions. Under these conditions a group is tempted to offer to the world a church, mistakenly purporting thereby to offer a faith. It is by this device that the extension of the church becomes its method of evangelism. It seeks to create disciples by adding persons to its church rather than by persuading those persons to participate in faith-response to divine overtures, then fashioning them into a church.

This confused manner of thinking naturally engenders in a church a *quantitative* standard for measuring its own strength. The "success pattern" of the community around it becomes also the index of the success of the congregation. Obviously it is easier to judge the size of a congregation than it is to estimate its spiritual realities. Items such as the affinities of its fellowship, the dynamics of its redemptive involvement — these are intangibles and do not lend themselves to exact measurement. The strength of the gospel which a church proclaims is not easily subjected to ordinary calculation. Yet, it is in terms of that gospel that any church deserves to be known. The question becomes, therefore, whether the significance of the church in the community is to be judged primarily in terms of its size. This is a judgment which the church itself is severely tempted to employ.

It is evident, upon reflection, that the essential ingredient of the gospel which is embodied in a large group can be said to be no stronger than that same gospel which is inherent in a smaller group. As a matter of fact, in both large and small bodies the gospel that is experienced and proclaimed is precisely the same gospel as that which has become effectual in *the faith-orientation of each member* of both groups. Unfortunately, this kind of yardstick is seldom employed in measuring the strength of the church. Like all other social entities the modern church is usually measured by the level of its success in competing for the persons and the material resources of the community. It is not often examined in terms of how extensively the spiritual verities of its value system have become infused, creatively, into the lives of the individuals and the private and public affairs of the neighborhood.

Frankly, when a church has become engrossed in a narcissistic, competitive process to the point that its chief concerns as well as its methods have become devoted to "getting" it has become selfish and self-centered, and selfishness is as conspicuous and despicable in a congregation as it is in an individual. A church which has become afflicted with this malady deserves to be "turned inside out," to be reconstructed so as to conform to the ideal of service for which it was intended.

As was indicated above, Christian faith and its concomitant character were placed in an awkward posture by developments in the culture which produced a sacred-secular schism. It was done, of course, to liberate non-church activities from the dominance of an imperial church but it has resulted in unfortunate consequences for both church and non-church endeavors. Besides virtually sealing off the church from the community in which it lives, it has encouraged the notion that all that is sacred in human life consists in some fashion in "doing something in and for the church." As a consequence it has become increasingly difficult to infuse into the workday responsibilities of mankind the motivation of the faith-values which normally characterize religious experience. Neither public policy nor the church has learned how to limit the activities of the institutional church without limiting also its spiritual values. By equating the internals and the externals of religion the entire province of faith becomes so identified with the institution it is difficult not to deny the free exercise of the value consciousness which religion inspires.

It is to be lamented that while immersed in the success atmosphere of the average community it is difficult for the church to maintain this distinction between its institution and its spiritual values. The extent to which the distinction is lost sight of is evidenced by the levels of *promotionalism* which have become characteristic of modern church groups. The merchandizing techniques of the marketplace are employed regularly and with evident success. Organizational aggrandizement achieved by the same methods as those employed by commercial establishments stands as a monument to the process. It remains to be seen, however, whether the verities of character formation and spiritual renewal lend themselves to the facile pressures of this kind of salesmanship.

This inordinate emphasis on the institutional, and the developments which furnished the church a virtual monopoly on things that are sacred have resulted in encouraging in the average congregation an elaborate system of "church activities." When a person "does his religion by work at the church," the church is quick to respond with a multiplicity of activities in which to engage its devotees. Like other social institutions churches continue to develop an elaborate system of auxiliary structures. This process, in turn, encourages the church to think of its own vitality in terms of the enlistment of its members in its organizational life. Modern churches administer "sacraments of activism." Activities have progressed to the point that to non-ecclesiastical members the activities promoted by the congregations approximate the level of significance for the individual that the sacraments enjoy in ecclesiastical groups.

This emphasis on "participation" in church affairs has become so intense that to refer to a person as being a "good churchman" now means that that person is "always there." This is vastly different from using the phrase, "good churchman," to mean that the individual is so committed in life to the meaning of the gospel that in every ramification of his life he conducts himself in a manner which is consistent with his faith-profession.

From its early history the church has engaged its members in "catechetical" studies, programs of instruction designed to familiarize them with the tenets of its faith. Free churchmen have given special emphasis to biblical studies because they have given such prominent place to the Bible as foundational to their faith. The biblical insights are so influential as case studies in revelatory inspiration free churches could scarcely overlook such study in their program of activities. In recent years the "Sunday School" has become an impressive organizational technique for Bible study and as a means of encouraging attendance at services of worship. With all of this emphasis on the Sunday School, however, it is instructive to bear in mind that the church managed to survive many centuries prior to the work of Robert Rakes in inaugurating the church school in the late eighteenth century.

Consistency would seem to require a church, whose prescription for the inception of a satisfactory religious experience is personal faith-response, to maintain as the conspicuous center of its life an altar of worship. As a matter of fact, a person's genuine worship may be said to consist essentially in *a continuation of his initial faith-experience*. It is a primary function of a congregation, therefore, to provide a time and place suitable for the worshipping individual. At frequent intervals every "faithing" person needs an arrangement wherein he may turn aside from the other activities of his daily routine so as to engage in worship. It becomes to him an occasion for clarifying his faith and for expressing it in sincere devotion.

The typical church that engages in a frenzied round of activities runs the risk of blurring its image in the community. To the extent it becomes a "busy" place it risks concealing from itself and from others its true nature as a worshipping community of believers. Each activity being maintained in these circumstances is able to justify its existence by the purposes it pursues. When taken together, however, all of the many "programs" can hardly be justified. Normally there is considerable overlapping in function. It is reasonable to think that if the total number should be reduced each probably would assume a much greater significance. Besides, any group so excessively active tends to consume its interests and energies in self-service, thereby neglecting the out-flow of its recreative spirit.

Evangelism is a primary dimension of the life of the church in the world. It consists in a church's effort to persuade, by the contagion of its spirit, all others to acknowledge the same sense of devotion as that which characterizes the church's membership. This sense of duty toward others is not solely in response to the expressed command of Christ which, within the perspective of those who are Christian, would be sufficient cause for mission. It is also the native inclination of any person who has come to view all things from the point of view of faith. It is an ultimate restlessness born of a sense of value which is inherent in the experience of faith itself.

This sense of duty was succinctly expressed by a rugged personality of the West Texas Plains who, upon becoming converted to Christianity in his middle years, declared that for only one brief moment in his Christian experience he had been perfectly content. When that moment had passed, he declared, he became peculiarly exercised in an interest in "Old Jim," a fellow cowboy of the Millet Cow Outfit in Throckmorton County, Texas. It occurred to him that "Old Jim" deserved to know the same satisfaction which had recently come to him. Normally, in any congregation of "faithers" there is a restlessness which radiates from its altar. It is like a "light set on a hill," an outreach of concern for those who do not know the way described as faith-orientation. The normal Christian perspective is evangelistic.

Unless a church is abnormally obsessed with a sense of otherworldliness it is *prophetic* in its posture in the world. Secure in its sense of Christian hope it, nevertheless, is sensitively aware of the conditions under which human life is lived in the world community. It is committed constantly and consistently to encouraging the good and to discouraging the evil in itself and in all it beholds. It subscribes to the notion that love is the character of the divine and deserves to become creative in all that is legitimate in the ratios of human affairs. As a matter of fact, to the Christian mind hope itself is a projection of this concept of love into a universal and eternal sovereignty.

Equipped with this sense of the power and effectual operation of love the believer engages in the so-called ordinary events of the marketplace, stirring patiently into its ebb and flow the motives with which his own life is inspired. He shares with all around him generous echoes of the character which to that point in his life he has achieved. His presence in the world becomes prophetic, therefore. Only by divesting himself of his name as a Christian and engaging in life in a manner which contradicts his profession can he avoid being a prophetic factor in the community.

When true to its profession a congregation lives by its vision of perfection. Even in its limited and imperfect fashion it strives always to create in every aspect of the world's life a condition of rectitude. It imposes upon the world an expectation of good. It imposes that expectation, not as an arbitrary demand it makes on the world but, instead, as an appeal to the moral sensitivity which it takes to be a constituent element in responsible human nature. It brings its expectation of good to that in human nature which is capable of making critical judgments between what is right and what is wrong. It appeals to the same element in human nature which, it believes, is a residual factor to which the incursions of the gospel can make appeal unto personal faith-response.

The church is committed to the judgment that the moral rectitude of the world is contingent upon directions which are determined by personal choice and the church believes devoutly that it has a responsibility to influence the choices persons make. It is bold to think that it is endowed with insights which can make a great deal of difference as to how personal choices are made. If true to its convictions regarding the differences between things as they are and things as they should be, it will exercise whatever power of persuasion it may possess in behalf of those moral imperatives which are decisive in all human equations. In a word, the church strives always to be prophetic.

A congregation which is humble in its concept of its convictions and endowments is proportionately less concerned about its own well-being and proportionately more involved as a catalyst of righteousness among men. It will exercise these concerns in seeking to persuade persons to make decisions according to the character and motivation by which the church itself lives. It will seek to be "salt for the earth," "leaven for the whole lump," a "light on a hill," "a plumb-line set among the people of the world." It will seek, not to call people away from the world, but to inspire in them the perspective of faith in God in